PSYCHIC DEFENSE
FOR YOGIS

PSYCHIC DEFENSE FOR YOGIS

A YOGIC MANUAL ON PSYCHIC PHENOMENA, PROTECTION, AND SELF-MASTERY

SWAMI NIRMALANANDA GIRI
(ABBOT GEORGE BURKE)

LIGHT of the SPIRIT
PRESS
CEDAR CREST, NEW MEXICO

Published by
Light of the Spirit Press
lightofthespiritpress.com

Light of the Spirit Monastery
P. O. Box 1370
Cedar Crest, New Mexico 87008
OCOY.org

ISBN-13 paperback: 978-1-955046-43-5
ISBN-13 epub: 978-1-955046-44-2

Library of Congress Control Number: 2026932433
Light of the Spirit Press, Cedar Crest, New Mexico

First Edition 2026

BISAC Categories:
1. REL032000   RELIGION/Hinduism/General
2. PHI015000   PHILOSOPHY/Mind & Body
3. REL062000   RELIGION/ Spirituality
4. OCC018000   MIND, BODY, SPIRIT/Psychic Phenomena/General
01232026

CONTENTS

INTRODUCTION

Do yogis need psychic defense? Most certainly–when the nature of psychic attack is understood. I want to speak about these two phenomena of psychic attack and psychic defense that are believed in by millions throughout the world but at the same time are never "in the public eye" because of the prevailing unbelief and skepticism of the people who shape public opinion and those who dislike thinking or speaking about anything negative or superstitious. In the motion picture "Dracula" with Bela Lugosi, the vampire hunter Dr. Van Helsing says: "The strength of the vampire is in the refusal of people to believe in him." This is true of all forms of evil.

It is a common occurrence that medical students develop the symptoms of the diseases they are studying. Although what I am going to tell you is accurate and not at all exaggerated, you must not let yourself become fearful and see danger lurking all around. Sometimes people get so absorbed in the idea of psychic attack that they forget there is psychic defense.

The most important principle in the consideration of psychic attack and psychic defense is to beware of both over-simplification and over-romanticizing. It is a serious mistake to cry "psychic attack" at every disturbance when, as Scrooge told Marley's ghost, it might just be "a bit of undigested cheese or underdone potato" that has been eaten, or some other alteration in body chemistry that we are experiencing. However, it is also a serious mistake to ignore the signals and be slow in determining the real state of things. I am saying this because caution and balance of mind are necessary lest our knowledge of these things degenerate into either baseless superstition or baseless skepticism.

First of all, what do we mean by "psychic," "psychic attack" and "psychic defense"? The word "psychic" refers to the subtle levels of our own nature and that of the worlds which metaphysicians call "astral" and "causal." These are very real levels of subtle energies that exist in us and all things in the material universe. The astral and causal levels and energies link us and the world of relative existence with the psychic levels which are above and separate from them. Each one of us is a complex entity consisting of four basic levels: spirit, causal energies, astral energies and matter. Except for spirit, which is consciousness, the other levels consist of vibrating energies of various sorts.

Since these simple facts are unknown to most people, most of the time psychic attack is not even recognized for what it is, and if it is, few people know how to shield themselves from it. For we are speaking of psychic defense, not counterattack.

Negative occultists and "magicians" love engaging in what they call "magickal wars." (The misspelling of "magical" indicates that they are to some degree followers of the notorious "magician" Aleister Crowley.) About thirty-five years ago someone contacted our ashram to warn us that a group of "magicians" in another state had "declared a magickal war" on us. We laughed. And that was the end of the matter.

However, psychic attack is a very real thing. I well recall sitting all night with a spiritual friend whom a very evil person was trying to murder by occult means. Another friend of mine had also fallen afoul of the same occultist and had nearly been killed by the attack. It was no joke—and very real.

Again I urge you to not become fearful, yet you should be aware that these things are real lest you become attacked and do not realize it. Many people think they are just "out of sorts" or "coming down with something" when they are actually being bombarded with destructive vibrations beamed at them by malicious people. On the other hand there are those who think they are "under attack" if they just get the flu or "feel funny." Hopefully what I am going to present will help you understand and be safe.

CHAPTER ONE

THE YOGI AND PSYCHIC PHENOMENA

What is a human being?

Perhaps the first step of our inquiry into psychic phenomena as they relate to the yogi is a definition of just what constitutes the human being and what constitutes psychic phenomena.

A human being consists of five layers–koshas, sheaths or bodies. These are, in ascending levels of subtle energies:

1) Annamaya kosha: "The sheath of food (anna)." The physical, material body, made of food.

2) Pranamaya kosha: "The sheath of vital air (prana)." The sheath consisting of vital forces and the (psychic) nervous system, including the karmendriyas.

3) Manomaya kosha: "The sheath of the mind (manas–mental substance)." The level (kosha) of the sensory mind. The astral body.

4) Jnanamaya kosha: "The sheath of intellect (buddhi)." The level of intelligent thought and conceptualization. Sometimes called the Vijnanamaya kosha. The astral-causal body.

5) Anandamaya kosha: "The sheath of bliss (ananda)." The causal body (karana sharira). The borderline of the Self (atman).

The pranamaya, manomaya and jnanamaya koshas together comprise the psyche, the psychic nature, of the human being. Psychic activity and perception take place in or through them. Someone in whom they are awake and active is a "psychic," and is aware of (and sometimes himself produces) psychic phenomena, which originate in the hidden regions of the mind.

In Genesis we are told: "And the Lord God formed man of the dust of the ground, and breathed into his nostrils the breath of life; and man became a living soul" (Genesis 2:7). Saint Paul wrote: "And so it is written, The first man Adam was made a living soul" (I Corinthians 15:45). The word Saint Paul used that is translated "soul," is psyche–the psychic levels of the human being. Adam, the first human being, was psychic. That is, his consciousness was centered in his psychic bodies rather than his physical body.

An adept yogi becomes aware of and fully functional in his psychic nature, which when purified and empowered by sadhana makes it possible for him to ascend into the consciousness of his spiritual nature his Self (Atman). In the Bible some psychic abilities are classified as gifts of the Holy Spirit.

The invisible worlds

The psychic faculty is invisible, and functions in the invisible realms. In those invisible realms there are various types of beings we may perceive or even communicate with. Some are negative, ignorant and foolish, and some are positive, knowledgeous and wise. Some are spiritually unevolved and others are highly evolved. We should not fall prey to the superstitious fear that even a slight peep into the psychic realm will bring demons crowding around ready to pounce on us—unless, of course, we are the kind of people who habitually associate with human "demons" and like their company. In that case their astral counterparts will be only too ready to contact us.

God is the creator of the invisible worlds as well as this visible one. In those, too, He is the supreme power, and His children need fear nothing therein, though as in this world caution is not a bad idea.

The Lord Jesus said: "In My Father's house are many mansions [mone: abodes]" (John 14:2). The invisible worlds are populated by many types of beings, busily pursuing their life. The mind of a psychically awakened and sensitive yogi is potentially an open window or door into those worlds. It is only natural that there may be a response from those that live there. The type of response will be determined by the psychic character of the observer and the responder. Therefore a person moving into the psychic world may be influenced by the intelligences he finds there. So the yogi must be able to tell which influences are desirable and which are not, and know how to resist and banish any undesirable influences.

Psychic attunement

A yogi puts his innate psychic radio or television into operation. Just as a radio or television set can only pick up the frequencies which it is programmed or built to receive, it is the same with the psychic faculty. It is our attunement, our state of psychic and spiritual evolution, which determines what worlds and what types of beings we will perceive.

Those who are old enough will remember the days when television was only VHF, so our sets only got the programs broadcasted on the VHF frequencies. Later when UHF broadcasts were introduced, we had to add on some equipment to enable our sets to pick them up. Also in those early days those of us who did not live in the cities where the broadcasts originated needed aerials with motors to turn them in the direction of the broadcast we wanted to receive. It took a lot of tuning and turning to get the picture. So it is with the psychic realms.

It is not enough to know that everyone has innate psychic abilities and can develop them. We must first see that our inner psychic "receivers" are rightly refined and attuned through spiritual practice, especially meditation. For the degree of our inner spiritual development will determine what inner psychic/astral levels/worlds we will contact and perceive.

Evil intelligences

Although I said we should not fear, I also said we needed wise caution. For there are negative spirits that have gotten stuck in the earth plane after death or somehow have wandered in from another dimension or world. Also, when Lucifer rebelled and was thrown from the heights of astral existence called "heaven," he and his unseen cohorts moved into the

lower regions, including this material plane, seeking to dom-
inate the worlds themselves and all who dwelt in them.

The evil intelligences under the leadership of Lucifer especially seek to influence the human mind. (See the book *Robe
of Light*.) Lucifer did not come to Eve and say: "Hello, I am
Lucifer. I am your enemy and I want to deceive you." Instead
he came to Eve and claimed to be her friend who wished to
give her the key to unlimited knowledge which would make
her like God. Here is the Biblical account:

"Now the serpent was more subtil than any beast of the
field which the LORD God had made. And he said unto
the woman, Yea, hath God said, Ye shall not eat of every
tree of the garden? And the woman said unto the serpent,
We may eat of the fruit of the trees of the garden: but of
the fruit of the tree which is in the midst of the garden,
God hath said, Ye shall not eat of it, neither shall ye touch
it, lest ye die.

"And the serpent said unto the woman, Ye shall not surely
die: for God doth know that in the day ye eat thereof, then
your eyes shall be opened, and ye shall be as gods, knowing
good and evil.

"And when the woman saw that the tree was good for food,
and that it was pleasant to the eyes, and a tree to be desired
to make one wise, she took of the fruit thereof, and did eat,
and gave also unto her husband with her; and he did eat. And
the eyes of them both were opened, and they knew that they
were naked" (Genesis 3:1-7), but had no remedy for their
nakedness, their vulnerability.

Things have not changed since then. There are evil, ignorant and foolish entities in the astral world—just as there are evil, ignorant and foolish people in this world—sitting at the gates and waiting for someone to poke their head through or enter. Just as we hear someone knocking at the door, so they perceive when a human being is trying to reach into their world. They will do what they can to "help" in hopes that in time the human being will be the means of their entering into the earth plane through obsession or possession. To ensure this they will lure the unsuspecting with phenomena of various sorts or at least make many promises that will remain unfulfilled once they attain their will.

Foolish and dangerous practices and phenomena

One very perilous practice is "automatic writing." The person sits with a pencil, or with a device called a planchette, and blanks his mind. After awhile his hand begins to move, and behold: he gets written messages "from the other side." (Mostly they are only from his subconscious mind.) After some time he may lose the ability to write anything on his own, and often starts writing against his will.

Other dangerous practices are those in which the individual becomes a psychic telephone or television set, either through "channeling" or through clairvoyant vision or by going into a trance state. The person eventually has no control over that, either. Sometimes he cannot have an uninterrupted conversation. He will be talking to somebody and in the midst of it say: "Oh, there is a little old man in the corner of the room. Was your grandfather named Benjamin?" As if the grandchild did not know the name of their grandfather! Then will come some inane stuff such as: "He used to take you fishing" or: "He loved taffy apples." Utter trivia, and what is already known.

The kind of non-human entities that usually are perceived are quite unintelligent, and like their human counterparts they never stop talking and they never say a single thing worth hearing. We all know humans like that, and there are spirits like that, as well. "Tell Edna the ink pen she lost twelve years ago was stolen by the milkman." "Ben must know that the back right tire on his car is going flat." "Helen is lying. I never told her she could have my best dishes when I was gone." The people who relay such drivel have no on/off switch, so it happens at any time. As I say, they are no more than telephones or television sets.

I remember a psychic in New Delhi trying to stop me at Connaught Circle to give me a "reading." "I know your mother's name," he told me. "So do I," I answered, and kept on walking. "But I can tell you your mother's name," he persisted, as he walked along beside me. "I can tell you her name, also. What will you pay me?" I asked him. "No, no, you do not understand! How is it that I know your mother's name?" "I don't know," I called back as I hastened away, "but a better question is just what you are going to do with such useless information."

Things get even worse with wandering spirits that are bored on the other side and want to get back here: a sure sign of ignorance. Unhappily the silly and the shallow think this kind of contact is wonderful.

Some entities are smarter, and they can tell us things we do not know, and even things that have a practical application. This is more dangerous, for they are clever enough to want more than mere relaying of messages.

There are truly vicious spirits who wish to invade our auras or bodies and live through us, defying the natural laws of rebirth. If they cannot possess someone permanently, they content themselves with short-term possession through their host's physical weakness, drunkenness or use of drugs. On a more formal and overt level they temporarily possess so-called "trance mediums." Or they draw the life-substance from the medium's body and create "materializations," the very touching of which can seriously harm the medium. These are the most degraded, immoral and criminal type of astral beings.

It must not be overlooked that oftentimes these phenomena are merely tricks of the medium's subconscious mind and there are no spirits whatsoever in contact with or through them. Their minds fake it all. But whichever it may be, deception is still deception and can only produce negative results.

Slaves of spirits

In the Bible those who mistakenly deal with such entities are warned away. There were certain people even in Biblical times that were "married" to spirits: linked irrevocably with them. In later times these entities were called "familiars." A television documentary once showed a Moslem woman of this type in the Middle East who every year on her "wedding" anniversary would kill a goat and smear herself with its blood in offering to her "husband." Such persons, being constant channels of evil and completely beyond correction, were condemned to banishment or death in the Old Testament. That may seem harsh, but when we understand the harm that is worked through them and the lack of adequate psychic defense against them it is comprehensible, though not the right reaction. Through the power of meditation and continual invocation of a mantra–especially Soham–such persons can be rendered harmless.

The positive side

We should also consider the positive side of the matter. For there is a very positive and beneficial mode of psychic communication and phenomena: the opening of the highest part of ourselves, our immortal spirit, to the world of God so that through our own evolution (not through the interference or action of other intelligences) the ability to perceive and function meaningfully on the higher psychic planes (and beyond) arises within us as a part of our own being and is wielded through our own divinely inspired and empowered will. That is, spiritualized psychic experience occurs as a natural consequence of our increasing level of evolution. The yogi becomes aware on many levels, including the psychic, even though that should never be his goal. The ultimate aim of his entire life should be Self-realization.

Revelation

Perhaps the most striking psychic record in the Bible is the book of Revelation in which the visions of Saint John the Apostle are recounted. They were spiritual communications transmitted through the purified psychic faculties of the Apostle. We know this is so, for he tells us: "I was in the Spirit on the Lord's day" (Revelation 1:10). He was not in his psyche, but in the spirit. Further, the term "Lord's day" means not just Sunday, but the eighth "day" or level of existence which transcends and yet embraces all the seven planes or modes of relative existence. In this way Saint John assures us that what he is about to tell us is coming from the highest point of consciousness that transcends all conditioned, relative states of consciousness. And what follows are symbols of spiritual realities, nearly all linked to yogic phenomena.

Moreover, we must not miss the point that everything Saint John tells us was his direct experience. He was not acting as a medium for any being, however high. He himself had ascended to the highest and witnessed all this directly. What he received he received directly from the Infinite. This is why none of the holy prophets of the Bible ever said: "Thus says my control," or "thus says my guide." Nor did they ever say: "Thus says the angel." Rather, they said: "Thus saith the Lord." For their spirits were in perfect union with the One Spirit; the finite was joined with the Infinite; the parts were one with the Whole. And so they spoke with the Divine Breath, the Holy Spirit.

Adam and Eve

Originally, Adam and Eve were citizens of the astral region of Paradise, functioning in that vehicle we call the astral body, which included their psychic faculties. For in the astral world all experience is psychic experience.

Eve could not distinguish between the Elohim, the Matrikas, the Creator Mothers, and Lucifer because she was not in touch with her higher, spiritual faculties that would have enabled her to perceive the difference. Also, Lucifer was an archangel and therefore likely to be mistaken for one of the Elohim. Eve was deceived through her psychic nature, something that would have been impossible if her awareness had been established in her spirit.

Not only did Lucifer look all right to Eve's psychic eye, so also did the astral fruit that brought about her psychic death. If she had looked with the eye of the spirit, she would have understood the nature of both and understood they were deadly: Lucifer because he was maleficent, and the fruit because she was not yet ready for the energies and the psychic opening they would convey. God meant for Eve to eat of the Tree of Knowledge, but not yet. She had only just come into Paradise and still had much development and learning ahead of her. If she had been back down on the earth and in the physical body, she could not have even seen or heard Lucifer; she would have been safe. But in Paradise she was susceptible to deception.

Our situation

Since we are ourselves "poor banished children of Eve," as
the prayer says, we are in the same predicament psychically.
Therefore it is indeed true that we must be cautious about the
psychic realms, and must endeavor to center our consciousness
in our spirit through meditation.

True intuition is spiritual intuition, not psychic intuition,
just as there is spiritual clairvoyance which is much higher than
psychic clairvoyance. It is crucial that we be aware of these
differences, because the merely psychic is often mistaken for
the spiritual. And although there can be errors in the psychic
realms, in the higher realms of the spirit only truth and higher
spiritual reality prevail. It is a natural part of evolution to
develop psychic faculties, but we must move on higher and not
become distracted by the merely psychic, though such lesser
experiences may come to us in our ascent to Self-realization.

Spiritual intuition is actually the higher faculty which
replaces the ordinary intellect as we ascend to spiritual perfec-
tion. But until we attain the highest awareness, much of what
we may mistakenly think is spiritual experience or phenomena
is really astral/psychic in character. That, too, is necessary for us,
but we must not get distracted or sidetracked, but must keep
pressing onward to the highest attainment of Self-realization.

As is usual with life, even spiritual life, the situation seems
contradictory. We must in time experience psychic phenomena
and perceptions, and yet must also be cautious regarding them
and understand that they, too, must be transcended as much as
material experience. We should think of our experience of the

psychic world as a journey. We must know the difficulties that may be encountered, the precautions that must be taken, and the mishaps and even dangers for which we must be prepared. We must know the danger zones and the safe zones. We must know the bad roads and the good roads. Yes, we must know them all. And we must make the trip and pass through them all. Without it there is stagnation. The same thing can be said of the development of consciousness as has been said about the American expansion into the West: "The cowards never started, and the weak died along the way." We must be neither.

Being safe and in control

What then should we do to ensure our safety in psychic matters? A principle that must be continually held in mind is the Biblical statement: "The spirits of the prophets are subject to the prophets" (I Corinthians 14:32). This implies that the higher, spiritual psychic abilities are the result of mastery of our inner faculties. And that mastery is the mastery that leads to the spirit–not short-sightedly to psychic experience as an end in itself. For though we must indeed journey through the realm of the psychic, we must go beyond it into total spiritual awakening, the realization: Soham–I Am That. (See *Soham Yoga: The Yoga of the Self.*)

The statement that the prophet's spirit is subject to him indicates that he is at all time fully in control of his inner life and experience. The opening of the psychic powers within the yogi comes as a result of spiritual evolution. This is why Blavatsky was insistent that ordinary, solely psychic abilities cannot be fully trusted. Rather, she insisted that only those who through spiritual cultivation open their own inner, illumined consciousness can trust their psychic perceptions or be trusted by others. Spiritual development is essential. Yoga is the way of authentic spiritual perceptions.

Two ways

In the world there are two types of supernormal contact: psychic and spiritual. We who are yogis must become increasingly more intent on the spiritual and less on the psychic side, not because there is anything wrong with the psychic but because it can sidetrack us in our quest for higher consciousness if we do not grow beyond it.

We must never confuse the psychic with the spiritual. It is common for people to think that psychics are spiritually developed when they are not, or that a psychic experience is a spiritual experience. When we do this we fall into two serious errors: we assume that because a psychic is accurate he is also a reliable spiritual advisor and guide, and we become satisfied with the psychic and neglect the spiritual–a logical consequence if we do not understand their difference. Psychic proficiency is not spiritual proficiency, and even miracles are no sign of spiritual worth in a person. There is a vast difference between psychic clairvoyance and spiritual clairvoyance and between all psychic and spiritual phenomena.

So please be aware that psychic advisors and healers are not spiritual advisors and healers. We must move onward to higher places as we evolve. The psychic world is normal and good, but the spiritual world is supernatural and of the highest value and meaning.

CHAPTER TWO

FORMS OF PSYCHIC ATTACK

What is psychic attack and what are its forms?

In essence, a psychic attack–or a psychic invasion, which is a close relative–is the incursion of negative energy or intelligence (one or more conscious entities) into an individual's energy fields–aura, etheric body, magnetic field, mental and emotional levels, etc. The labels are not important, the fact of invasion is. Keeping this definition in mind, let us consider various types of psychic attack.

1) Encountering wandering bands or fields of "natural" negative energies.

As winds circle the earth, so there are energy currents circulating worldwide as well, some of which can have negative effects on the individual's physical or psychic nature. This is especially common in our days of nuclear energy and other deadly radiations and substances. Often what a person experiences is simply an echo of some negative or unbalancing event in the earth's magnetic field. Of course, often it is purely physical, a result of some type of atmospheric pollution.

Just as sound moves through the atmosphere, so also do negative emotional vibrations. We may be struck by wandering clouds of negative energies released by anger and violence from those around us or in our neighborhood. A husband and wife may have an argument and even strike one another. Then the evil magnetism emanating from their auras detaches itself and floats around like a malevolent cloud until it is absorbed by a person or object whose aura is susceptible or defenseless, or who is also vibrating with similar anger.

It is not uncommon for people to walk through a crowded building and come out feeling somewhat ill–especially with a headache. Sometimes when sitting in the supposed safety of our homes we suddenly feel the onslaught of anxiety, depression, fear or other negative states. Walls are not always defenses against the wandering clouds of released malevolent energies or intelligences.

Traffic seems to evoke the most violence in people. It is not uncommon for someone's car to develop a problem after some fellow driver has released a burst of anger at them for some supposed driving offense.

Armed conflicts produce tidal waves of such energies and sweep over the face of the earth catching others up into their poisonous vortexes. In psychic levels, especially, "no man is an island."

Certain places can also be gathering points for various types of destructive energies. Hospitals, mental institutions and prisons head the list, closely followed by "adult" motion picture theaters and stores and sexually-oriented "clubs."

Unhappily, certain churches that capitalize on hatred and fear are power centers of negativity and radiate a very real psychic poison.

(2) The effect of coming in contact with negative, deadening, or destructive energy fields emanating from physical substances or objects—either by innate nature or through magnetization by someone, intentionally or unintentionally.

Heading the list of this type would be contact with radio-active materials, which are not only dangerous from the simple standpoint of radiation, but they weaken the psychic fabric of the earth plane and permit or produce "bleed over" or outright invasion from negative psychic planes. Also, some substances bear very definite anti-life vibrations or attract anti-life entities. Low "magic" uses poisonous and disgusting substances because they vibrate on the anti-life wavelengths of death and decay. Certain types of entities are also attracted to substances in a state of breakdown so they can draw off the released energy. Shed blood and reproductive fluids are in this category.

Certain malevolent people like to implant such substances in the bodies or environments of intended victims. They may often take a perfectly innocent object and subject it to ritual defilement so it will be a channel for evil power. Sometimes this is not a conscious act on the part of negative individuals who have no formal knowledge of occult principles, but just by handling an object with intense thought or feeling they turn it into a vehicle for negativity.

Often evil people give their victims some object which then acts as a link between them and the person. The only solution is for the victim to destroy the object, get rid of it or neutralize the magnetization and then bless it. Here is an example.

Once a woman came to our ashram asked if I would bless her house. She had married a man whose mother was an overt sorceress in an Eastern European country. After she came on a visit to them, everything went wrong between the husband and wife and even with the house. So strong was the malevolence that the husband gave up and divorced our friend, hoping in that way to at least get his mother's curse off of him. After the divorce things calmed down, but our friend felt that something was still not right, and asked if I thought a house blessing would help. Since it is a good thing to bless a house in all circumstances I suggested that one be done.

Along with another monk I went and blessed the house, which had a very normal atmosphere right from the first. Because of this I assumed there was no problem. Right at the end of the blessing I asked the woman to open the doors of a glass-fronted cabinet where I could see many items of china displayed. "Oh!" she exclaimed, "my mother-in-law gave me those. She brought them from Europe and made a big point about my having them." "Then I know they should be blessed," I replied. She tried to open the doors and found them locked. "But I never lock them," she said. It took a while to find the key, but she managed. The moment the blessed water touched that china a tremendous negative force exploded out of them, terrifying our friend and certainly impressing us. In a moment the force was gone, literally running out the door. So all was well from then on. The potential harm had been defused. What exactly had been done to the dishes was unknown, but they had become a nest of deadly power.

Be wary of supposedly blessed or magnetized objects whose source of blessing is unknown to you. Not all blessings really are blessings. Sometimes the "blessers" are negative or foolish people who intentionally or unintentionally impart negative or unbalanced energies to objects and places.

Once I visited a yoga center which had psychic disturbances. Several people had seen spirits there, as well. The head of the center told me about the situation and asked me to go through the building and see if there was anything I could sense about it. I did so, and found nothing. So I walked around the building. When I came to the back door I found tacked to it a block print of a complex tantrik diagram that had been given to the center. That was the problem. They took it down, burned it, and everything was all right immediately. No doubt the person that gave it to them did so in good faith, thinking that it was a spiritual object and therefore would impart positive vibrations.

(3) Bombardment of negative personal thoughts or emotions emanating from another person, intentionally or unintentionally.

This is the most common type of psychic attack. Some people consciously radiate negative vibrations, but most do it quite unconsciously, and have no idea they are broadcasting negative energies to the people and places around them.

Contributing to the effectiveness of this type of attack is its not being identified as such. For when we say "psychic attack," we think of someone in magical robes hurling curses from a tower in a crumbling castle. But we do not give any consideration to common, nasty thought vibrations that can penetrate our auras and surroundings and affect us.

On a much smaller scale, you can experience an unintentional psychic attack from someone who becomes angered at you for some reason and swears or rails at you, either aloud or in their mind.

(4) Experiencing the consciously directed negative energies methodically produced by esoteric means (magic, etc.) and sent forth specifically or generally.

Yes, it is true—there are those people who use occult means to injure and even destroy others. This is very real, and not to be discounted one bit. Some of them actually make a living as psychic assassins. Sometimes the psychic attacks launched by such evil ones are not with a special individual in mind, but are directed against either humanity in general or against certain groups or types of people. The effects are just as harmful, however.

(5) Invasion by another intelligence, usually disembodied, either by its own volition or under the command of another will.

Earthbound souls, especially those of a negative character, can cause psychic disturbance.

The presence of ignorantly or willfully harmful entities in the earth plane–usually called in by evil occultists–is a tragic fact. These wanderers, for a variety of motivations, often seek to invade human beings, their homes or environment, either to possess their bodies, feed off their energies (they are especially attracted to the auras of those who use alcohol, nicotine, or drugs), or simply to experience some type of contact with another intelligence. Whatever the motives, the results are always harmful to some degree.

It is definitely true that some workers of evil make use of "familiar spirits" who are invoked and bound by them and sent to work their will–often to injure and even destroy. Some create evil "robots" of negative thought, emotion, and will energies to accomplish the same intentions. (It sounds insane when stated so baldly, but that is because the act is insane.) Sometimes the purpose of these entities is to seduce us into their ways, as well. These may appear to their targets and use psychokinetic force and other external manifestations.

Certain occult initiations produce obsession by spirits. The auric invasion of such beings can produce mental illness and even suicide. Sincerity of intention is no sure safeguard in these matters. One particularly foolish but nevertheless harmful "spiritual" group actually promises its prospective candidates that after their initiation an "elemental" spirit will be permanently imbedded in their aura.

There are all kinds of entities that can bother people, but the most commonly (because easily) employed entities by negative or foolish occultists are the spirits called "elementals." An elemental is a type of low-developed nature spirit, not very intelligent but possessing definite powers. Without their understanding the nature of the situation, they often become a kind of servant/slave of an occult individual or group and are sent to bother a designated person or persons.

There are four kinds of elementals: earth elementals, water elementals, fire elementals and air elementals. They are too unintelligent to know that what they are doing is attacking, they just "do" what they are told. (I have no idea how they are told to do it by those who send them.) Elementals have no concept of either injury or death.

Earth elementals make their targets feel heavy, depressed, tired and mentally inert, even vegetative. Water elementals make people feel confused, vague, unsure and weak. Fire elementals make people feel restless, nervous, jittery, hyperactive, volatile, easily angered and even violent. Air elementals make people feel mentally and physically numb, spacey, mentally and emotionally unsure, compulsive, and of course flighty.

When elementals do not succeed in their mission, and especially if they become disturbed or feel resisted, or even "burned" by their target invoking higher vibrations that can banish them, they become confused and angry. When that happens their target or anyone around them often smell the vibration of their confusion and anger. So if you should do so, know that an elemental has been thwarted in attempting to harm you. Earth elementals produce a smell like an open sewer or septic tank which also has a powerful metallic, almost caustic, overtone. Water elementals produce a smell like fish (sometimes decaying fish). Fire elementals produce a smell like burning tobacco smoke. Air elementals produce a smell like either wet, decaying leaves, stagnant water, ozone or chlorine.

Although elementals are sent to do harm, when they become disturbed or angry they often stop their attack and return to their senders and may do them very real harm–which they deserve.

6) Auric invasion by others through physical touch

Our etheric body extends about an inch from our physical body. Psychically sensitive people can sometimes see it as a light or halo around someone's body. I once gave a talk at a psychic fair about psychic attack. At one point I asked the sponsor of the fair to come stand by me. I then just put my hand on his shoulder and told the people, "I am now in his etheric body, and will be so as long as I am touching him. So beware and 'be wary' of anyone you do not know–or some you do know–touching you like this. Huggers and strokers are invading you. Do not allow it unless you know them well and know their intentions are positive. It is the same with shaking hands. In just a few moments you can be invaded and affected by shaking hands. And never let someone you do not know well keep holding your hand. Those who take your hand, look in your eyes and keep speaking to you are totally invading you. Their intentions may not be bad, but be wary.

You cannot avoid shaking hands sometimes, but consciously resist any influence."

7) Invasion through food

When food is cooked its vibration is changed and it absorbs the bio-energies of whoever cooks it or serves it. This is why in traditional Indian households there are many rules about food and its consumption. They all have a very real basis.

You can absorb the mental energies of the cook in a restaurant, for example. My friend, Dr. A. K. Bhattacharya, the son of Dr. Benoytosh Bhattacharya, the father of modern radionics, told me that he was unable to eat any food but that cooked by his wife or daughter. One time a very close friend who was warden of a prison invited him for lunch. He broke his rule and went there to eat. The food was especially good tasting, but when he returned home he felt pervaded by negative energies that were even violent. He had never raised his voice to his wife in their entire marriage, but he did so shortly after returning home. This shocked him. Pondering the matter he thought it might have been the food he ate. So he telephoned his warden friend and asked who had cooked the food. The warden told him that one of the prisoners, an excellent cook who had been diagnosed as criminally insane, had cooked it!

Another not uncommon form of psychic invasion through food is done by someone taking food from their plate and putting it on yours, saying: "Oh! Try some of this. It is very good." Many negative or chronically ill people do this frequently, for in this manner they are passing their negative or disease energies on to you. Also, some people often take food from your plate, saying: "May I try some of that?" They are taking your positive or healthy vibrations. Those who habitually swap food in this way are trading their negative vibrations for your positive vibrations. Do not allow this. When very close friends or family members do this it can be harmless. But if it is continual, then know something is wrong and stop it.

Places susceptible to psychic invasion

Houses and other buildings are powerful thought-forms. Since they are built with the idea of closing out undesirable things it is not easy for negative energies to invade them. (Remember the belief that a vampire has to be invited into a house?) But certain areas of a building are weak in this way and negativity may enter through them. They are corners, closets, attics, and basements. Corners are not walls, but are a kind of "no-man's-land," so entities and energies that cannot pierce a wall can sometimes penetrate a corner. For some reason the northeast corner of a building or a room is particularly vulnerable to this kind of psychic invasion. For that reason the Russian Orthodox Christians often hang an icon across the northeast corner of a room. Closets, attics, basements–and sometimes bathrooms–are susceptible to invasion because they are not really parts of the house intended for human habitation, but are a sort of psychic "no-man's land." So they, too, become neutral territory and liable to psychic penetration.

CHAPTER THREE

SYMPTOMS OF PSYCHIC ATTACK

(1) Vague unease, a sense of something indefinable being wrong or about to happen

This is usually the initial symptom of a psychic attack. You cannot put your finger on what it is, but something just does not feel right. There is a kind of nagging at the back of your mind. What I am describing may not be an intense feeling, but one so slight and subtle that you are often hardly aware you are experiencing it. In fact, if you are busy or intent on some train of thought it may be a while before you come to realize that for some time a peripheral area of your mind has been experiencing this type of unease.

The usual way this develops, when it is really the symptom of a psychic attack, is this:

(a) A slight feeling that something is not quite right—a feeling you might get if something was out of place or missing from a familiar room. This is followed by:

(b) An unsettling feeling of vague apprehension, the "prick-ling of the hairs on the back of the neck"—but so subtle, so almost subliminal that it barely registers until (as it will) it grows into a more perceptible feeling that something is definitely wrong. Some people do not feel fear or apprehension, but instead experience this as a feeling of intense restlessness or the jitters. (Parents should be very careful about reprimanding their children for being hyper or extremely restless and rushing around unable to calm down. Often they are experiencing a psychic attack that their parents are unaware of. They may even be absorbing the energies of an attack that is directed at the parents but is deflecting onto them.)

(c) Because of the tension produced by this, headache or other mild symptoms of tension may result. When this happens, the person rationalizes that their first feelings of unease must have been indications of a developing physical problem, and so the possibility of detecting the psychic attack is very unlikely. Also, a person often attributes the symptoms of illness to the strain of being unable to figure out what is going on—often for the very purpose of providing a reasonable explanation. This is especially true of very intellectual-rational personalities.

On the other hand, if the above-described process does not take place, the next step is usually:

(2) Baseless fear, sometimes even escalating into terror

This is one of the worst symptoms of psychic attack, for not only is it terrible to experience, it also destroys the objectivity of the mind, causing it to relinquish its defenses and becoming even more susceptible to negativity.

Fear opens the aura, rendering the person utterly defense-less, and therefore almost totally in the power of the attacking forces, for fear truly is paralyzing, as we often say. Moreover, being gripped by fear, the individual becomes frantic and con-fused—therefore unable to realize the source of the problem.

Often a mistaken conclusion is that the problem is psycho-logical. The person may even go so far as to get medication to deaden his sensitivity to the attack. Some of these drugs in turn open the psyche even more to outside psychic influence, though physically they appear to shut down the individual. Caught in this vicious cycle, the person may become tempo-rarily or permanently more susceptible to evil forces.

However, there is a piece of knowledge that when kept in mind can mean the difference between immunity and full surrender to a psychic attack: At the onset of the psychic attack, it is not genuine fear which you feel, but rather, the purely physical sensation of apprehension or fear. That is, you are not really afraid at first, but you feel afraid. Sometimes this is because the attacking energies penetrat-ing your aura and body are causing your adrenal glands to respond in defense. But most of the time it is a deliberate implanting of a false experience of fear with the intention of producing real fear in you. This usually works, since few people are able to experience their feelings objectively, and so from the feeling of fear, actual fear arises. This is the deceit of the evil forces: by making you feel afraid, they make you become genuinely fearful, and therefore helpless before them. So when you find yourself feeling fearful or apprehensive without a cause, realize that you perhaps are being bombarded by destructive energies and take steps to protect yourself.

As you can see so far, the major difficulty in the matter of psychic attack is our frequent inability to recognize it for what it is and then act accordingly and defend ourselves.

Although fear is the most common–because the most effective–emotion resulting from psychic attack, another symptom is:

(3) Negative emotions which in general have no basis

Naturally, we all get irritated on occasion, or disgusted, or repelled by various situations. And sometimes our negative emotions seem to come from nowhere or have no basis when they are instinctive defense reactions against the unknown. But there are times when irrational feelings of anger, resentment, dislike or infatuation and desire (we tend to miss the fact that positive or attracting emotions can also be manipulations from psychic attack), etc., are produced in us as a result of a psychic attack–again, usually as physical sensations at first, which then turn into the actual mental states.

Often we condemn a person for their unreasonable emotional outbursts, labeling them immature or unstable, when they are the victims of psychic attack and need protection. We must always be thinking of what we can do to rectify a situation–not to just put a label on it and pass by like those in the parable of the Good Samaritan who would not help the wounded man.

Depression and feelings of helplessness are common manifestations of psychic invasion. And, like all these others, such
states are automatically interpreted by us as mere psychological
difficulties and therefore not diagnosed or treated correctly.
Here, too, people often resort to medications that only com-
pound the problem or create another.

Again, be aware that emotions of intense attraction and
desire can also be effects of psychic attack. Many leaders, both
political and religious, have strong powers of domination which
manifest in their victims as intense loyalty (even love) and
devotion for them. I have been in the presence of people who
in actuality were shallow, ignorant and outright unintelligent
(as was Hitler), yet they could cast such a "glamor" over the
minds of the people in the room that they appeared wise and
worthy of being followed to the death. The disciple of one
contemporary "guru" once remarked to me that whenever he
spoke to the "master" about any problem he felt he was being
given great wisdom in return, and would be overwhelmed with
feelings of exaltation and gratitude. But the moment he left
the room or building, he realized that the things said to him
were actually inane, and often stupid and pointless. I knew
a yogi who could get people to do completely idiotic things.
Whatever he said or ordered seemed perfectly right and sensible
to them. Later they would be astounded at having agreed to his
directions. This was a result of his psychic domination of them.

I think we have all had dreams in which something seemed
either very profound or very funny, but upon awakening we
realized that it made no sense at all or was a commonplace

thought without any special wit or wisdom. This is because we were in a subconscious state when we experienced it. So also, psychic attack is mostly on the subconscious level, and when we are under its influence our evaluations can be totally false. Also, since they are subconscious, the effects of psychic attack can be very like post-hypnotic suggestions.

Some people under psychic attack become a type of awake sleepwalker with their perceptions completely distorted, even seeing, hearing and feeling completely at the will of the one attacking them. They will see words on a page that are not there, will see figures or hear sounds that are not real, and will feel emotions not their own. These cases are often not simple matters of psychic influence by a person, but the result of obsession by evil spirits–for a human occultist would quickly burn out from the intensity of effort required to sustain this state in another. However, the obsessing entity may be under the command of some malevolent person, and will have been specifically sent by him to produce this state in the victim.

This phenomenon is most commonly encountered when entire groups are under the influence of a particular person or emotion. This includes highly emotional religious gatherings. Usually the invasion of the entity comes from the victim being either personally "blessed" (or even "exorcised"!) by the attacker(s). I knew a man who could make anyone "talk in tongues" by simply touching them on the back of the neck where the chakra that controls speech is located.

Politics runs a close second with religion in psychic domination and delusion.

Sincerity of intention is no sure safeguard in these matters.

(4) Nausea, headache, inexplicable pains (usually sharp)

Although headache and minor pains were mentioned before as results of the mind's tension at being unable to understand what is going on in a psychic attack, many pains are direct effects of psychic attack, often being the results intended by the attacker. The most common conception of psychic attack is the "voodoo doll" with pins stuck in it to produce pains in the victim. This is not mere fantasy, though a doll or image is not necessary for this kind of attack. The pains are usually of the "shooting" kind, though "the spike through the head" sensation is not uncommon. (I knew a woman who was expert in this kind of attack just for her own malicious amusement and the need to feel powerful and superior to others.) Migraine-like attacks are often psychically induced. On occasion the pains and nausea are products of the energy imbalance that result from the alien energies entering the victim's body and overloading it.

(5) Mental confusion, mental inertia, inability to think clearly or understand or comprehend what is going on

Psychic attack often affects us like a blow on the head or a slap in the face—it completely disorients us and keeps us from getting our bearings. This, of course, produces a feeling of helplessness, which then results in fear or anxiety which then breaks down any defenses we might have. Also, part of a psychic attack often is the deliberate prevention of our being able to realize what is happening to us. Often, this state is produced in us to keep us from accomplishing something the evil forces do not want done. This is often tied up with:

(6) Irrational feelings of exhaustion, listlessness, heaviness, and energy drain. Conviction of the inability to do anything

This is very common. And it is almost never combatted because of its mundane, unspectacular character. Not being a painful experience, and by its very dullness not fitting in with our glamorous thunder-and-lightning image of what a psychic attack is, we usually accept this as being the true state of things, figuring that we have not been sleeping well lately, or that we need to eat better, etc.

When you think of something you need to do, it can seem like a tremendous task, a herculean labor that you just do not have the stamina or energy to carry through. It seems completely beyond you, either impossible or requiring more effort or trouble than you want to expend. Even though intellectually you know how easy and virtually effortless the task or project may be, it will loom in your mind as something requiring overwhelming effort. This is hypnosis of a sort, and incredibly dangerous.

Alternately, you may feel drained of all energy, worn out, and weighed down, even though you have done nothing that could have resulted in such a dramatic loss of energy or fatigue. The enemy is trying to trick you into inaction so he can work unhindered while you "rest up." Beware!

(7) Flashing of hypnogogic images. You keep "seeing things" out of the corner of your eye, or dream-type images keep flashing before you, especially when you are sitting or relaxed

Frequently you get the impression of objects flying past your head, as if thrown at you. If you tend to be clairvoyant, you will experience this very clearly, even ducking to avoid being hit. Or you suddenly feel that some person or thing is lunging at you. Often these experiences are just mental blips whose very insubstantiality makes you tend to disregard them or pass them off as a symptom of fatigue or "brain fag." This type of attack has two purposes: (a) to feed into your mind images of yourself being injured in some way (usually violently), of being seriously ill, or even of being dead or dying. If accepted, these images can be turned into actualities or else used to produce terrible fears or paralyzing convictions of impending disaster in you. Or, (b) they are meant to frighten you by making you think you are hallucinating and perhaps going crazy, or to make those around you think you are mentally unbalanced (especially if you flinch or cry out when you see things flying past you).

On occasion, though, these are not images being sent to you by an attacker, but are instead the signaling of your subconscious mind that you are under a psychic attack. Since the subconscious deals in pictures and not words, it sends you images of disaster and injury to alert you. What it shows you may not be the literal intentions of the attacker, but just a general message. For example, if the attacker wants you physically injured, you may see all kinds of pictures of accidents or assault. The actual pictures do not matter—it is the theme of injury. The attacker might want you to break a leg, but your mind would show you all kinds of images, from being hit by a train to falling in a hole. So do not take the images as literal prophecies of coming events. The thing is to realize that you are being attacked, though for some reason you are not picking up on it, and your inner mind is signaling you to defend yourself.

Do not discount the reality of such imagery even if the images seem silly or memories of old horror movies you have seen. Malevolent people often send images of movie monsters and such like to their intended victim's mind so the victim will not take them seriously, or so that anyone they tell about their experiences will think they are fools or crazy. This is not speculation. I once read a book that gave instructions about this very kind of mental persecution. Some years later I met a man who told me that at one time in his life he would actually see Frankenstein's monster. He laughed about it while telling me because he did not realize its nature and purpose.

(8) Symptoms of illness, but no actual problem detectable

This is particularly insidious, because the victim can die with family and physician swearing it is "all in his head." Or at best the person endures much suffering which, when it disappears, only strengthens the mistaken conviction that "there was nothing to it." Since we tend to let others shape our opinions about ourselves, this type of thing can cause us to lose confidence in our own perceptions and experiences. And that can be as disastrous as overconfidence.

But the most important thing about this symptom is that it usually indicates an attempt at psychic murder. (Do not think that such things are impossible–I have witnessed them). There have been cases where psychic assassins have produced the symptoms of diseases so the medical treatment itself would kill the victim.

I have witnessed this, also. In one case the assassins produced false symptoms of lymphatic cancer in a man. Chemotherapy was administered, which the man barely survived. Then the doctor declared that the man had not had cancer at all, but that he wanted him to have more chemotherapy "to make sure." Such outrageous stupidity was of course the result of psychic influence on the doctor's mind. The second bout of chemotherapy destroyed the victim's natural immunities. He caught a respiratory flu that was going around and became unable to even walk. His family members had to carry him into the doctor's office. The doctor–again under evil psychic influence–told him he was fine and to quit being a hypochondriac. After some days he went into a coma and convulsions, so his family had him taken to a hospital. The doctor came, expressing great anger at "all this fuss about nothing." Seeing the man's condition, even psychic influence could no longer blind him to the seriousness of the matter. However, he refused to accept that the problem was respiratory, but announced that the man had "Laetrile poisoning." Now, this was most interesting, since the family preferred alternative therapies and in the past had successfully used Laetrile, though the doctor did not know that. The psychic assassins knew, however, and worked to produce the symptoms of cyanide poisoning, hoping that the family would have given him Laetrile. Then not only would the victim die, the family could be indicted for manslaughter and go to jail, as well. The doctor had tests run, which showed no traces of Laetrile. Then he at last conceded that the problem was respiratory, but began to pressure the family to "let him die in peace," and "why run up a big bill by putting him in intensive care?" It was as though the doctor (under negative psychic influence) wanted the man to die. Ultimately the man was killed by the supposed treatment, as one of the hospital staff later confessed to the family.

(9) Sudden illness with no prior basis, often from an encounter with a worker of evil

This type of illness is the kind that used to be attributed to the "evil eye." This is a tricky one, because we do not want to be like the medieval farmers who blamed witches every time their cows got sick. Still, the possibility must be kept in mind.

The usual revealing factor in this type of psychic attack is the incredible suddenness of the illness and the intense virulence of it. Most illnesses develop, but psychically induced ones often strike like lightning–unless the attacker is particularly clever and realizes that unless he takes his time someone may be alerted to the real nature of the illness. The usual strategy, though, is to kill the victim before any force can be rallied against it.

A perfectly healthy attorney went into court against some criminals who had connections with psychic assassins. The atmosphere was truly hellish in the courtroom, and when the attorney came away he was barely able to walk. Within a few hours he could not walk, and had to be taken by ambulance to a hospital where he was found to have advanced rheumatoid arthritis. He eventually died. One of his legal partners took up the case, and in less than a week was taken to the hospital with a strange blood disease that could not be identified or (therefore) treated. Prayer–intense prayer–saved his life, but in just a day or so the third partner, who was in excellent health, was stricken with an unidentifiable kidney ailment and nearly died within eight hours. Only their accidental learning of his problem enabled the "prayer people" to get to work and save him. The next day he was perfect–and the doctors were mystified. The cure was swift because of prayer being brought to bear so quickly. The partner with the blood disorder took several weeks to completely clear up, because prayer had not been brought into the picture until nearly two weeks after the appearance of the "illness."

(10) Disturbances in the near environment, especially electrical burnout and malfunction

When negative energies directed at us do not or cannot enter our auras, they often ricochet off and strike persons or objects in our immediate locale. Other people, or animals, may pick up the symptoms intended for us. This is true of inanimate objects, as well. Inexplicably, machinery that has always functioned well may break down. This is especially true of electrical problems, for psychic attack is directed at the human nervous system, and the electrical system of a house or machine is, in a way, its nervous system.

One man had two cars, a lawnmower, and several household appliances burn out in three days. At the same time both his wife and a hired worker had to be taken to the hospital. He asked me what might be the matter, and I explained that it was definitely a psychic attack. Being knowledgeable about esoteric things, he realized the truth of my diagnosis and set to work correcting matters and had no more troubles.

Again, we must not attribute everything that goes wrong to a psychic attack, but we must not ignore the possibility, either.

(11) Hallucinations

As mentioned before, visual and auditory hallucinations may be symptoms of psychic attack.

(12) Smells

However outlandish it may seem, occasionally, as already mentioned, psychic attacks are accompanied by smells, or to be more exact, the types of energies or entities used by the attacker may produce a distinctive smell. I want to repeat here what I said before.

Disturbance or presence of earth elements known as gnomes may produce a smell like a sewer or septic tank has been opened. Yet, there is no mistaking this awful smell for that of a real septic tank, for its predominant characteristic is a powerful metallic, almost caustic, overtone which does not occur in nature. However, the excrement of an obsessed or possessed person may have this same smell, and is one of the traits by which a diagnosis of obsession or possession may be confirmed. I have encountered this twice. Hopefully you will never have to experience it, but once you do, you will know well what it is.

Interestingly enough, the presence of fire elementals known as salamanders (not the lizards) may be known by a smell like burning tobacco.

A smell like wet leaves, stagnant water or a "fishy" smell, is produced by the presence of water elementals known as undines.

A smell like ozone or chlorine indicates the presence of air elementals known as sylphs.

Along with the smells of elementals you can sometimes pick up the "feeling," or vibration, of the person who is behind the attack.

(13) Depression

This is not so much the depression that results from being disappointed in others or in a life situation, but the type of depression in which the person feels he is worthless or help-less—in other words, a depression that produces a belittling self-image. For the attacker is wanting to convince the victim that he is nothing, and therefore helpless. Isolation is the key note of this type of depression, as well.

Usually the attacker simply wants to reduce the victim to inactive, psychic jelly, but occasionally urges to suicide will also accompany the depression. This latter type of depression is usually accompanied by bursts of violence that at first may be directed towards others, but eventually turns into self-violence.

(14) Addiction

Addiction—especially to alcohol, drugs, and sex—is frequently a result of psychic attack or psychic invasion. Often earthbound spirits that were addicted to those things in their previous life, and are still obsessed with them, invade the aura of a person and continually urge them through their subconscious minds to use those things. Homicidal maniacs often enter someone's aura and incite them to violence and even murder. People who after years of normal life suddenly "discover" that they have abnormal sexual proclivities have usually been invaded by a perverted spirit that is driving them toward aberrative behavior.

In sum

From all this you should be able to correctly diagnose whenever you or others are under psychic attack.

All these people described desperately need psychic defense.

Susceptibility to Psychic Attack

Certain substances in your body make you more susceptible to psychic attack, such as meat, alcohol, nicotine, or other drugs. Avoid them assiduously. Also, do not be constipated, as the buildup of toxic waste in the body also increases your susceptibility. All these things I have listed are attuned to the vibrations of death and can even draw negative energies and entities to you.

During the time of a psychic attack, it is good to eat something every few hours, such as root vegetables or grains, which stabilize the energy body, for fasting increases your sensitivity to psychic forces in general, and during time of psychic attack a little positive desensitization does no harm.

Most important: one of the best exorcisms and defenses is a good laugh. I once read that the world's most powerful black magician could have no effect on someone who was sitting in a theatre laughing at a comedy.

Almost as important as laughter is good, positive company. When you have done what you can to counter a psychic attack, go find some cheerful people with whom you can enjoy yourself, and be with them.

The greatest of defenses is prayer. If you are praying or reciting a true spiritual prayer or mantra your aura will be impenetrable—unless you need to be made aware of the attack or have some lesson to learn or karma to reap.

Often negativity within ourselves opens us up to psychic attack, so examine your own conscience, your thoughts, emotions, and deeds, and see if you need some inner housecleaning to make yourself strong against evil.

Remember that preventive medicine is the best medicine, and be always strong in your spiritual life.

CHAPTER FOUR

DEFENDING AND STRENGTHENING YOURSELF

God is light, and in him is no darkness at all (John 1:5).

God, being Light in which there is no darkness, there can be no mightier or more effective defense in any situation whatsoever than the invocation of Higher Consciousness. This is because evil–darkness–does not really exist as an entity in itself. Rather, it is merely a lack, an absence of Light and Truth–of God. God being effectively invoked, evil is no more. For it never was. Therefore sacred thoughts and sacred objects are the perfect defense against all evils.

On the previous page I said a rather amazing truth: "If you are praying or reciting a true spiritual prayer or mantra your aura will be impenetrable." There are many sacred mantras that became known to the sages of India through their inner research into the things of the spirit–the divine Self (Atman) of every human being. But the supreme mantra that embodies the highest consciousness and enlightenment is Soham. (Again, see the book *Soham Yoga: The Yoga of the Self.*)

Soham

"In the beginning was the Word, and the Word was with God, and the Word was God" (John 1:1).

Sound is the foundation of the universe, of all existence. Everything is vibrating energy, and that energy in its essential nature is sound. The Primal Sound, the root vibration that is manifesting as everything that exists, is the sacred mantra Soham. Soham (which is pronounced like "Sohum") means: I Am That. It is the natural vibration of the Self, which occurs spontaneously with each incoming and outgoing breath. Through becoming aware of it on the conscious level by mentally repeating it in time with the breath (*So* when inhaling and *Ham [Hum]* when exhaling), a yogi experiences the identity between his individual Self and the Supreme Self.

There are mantras that change things and others that reveal the eternal nature of things. Soham does both. Soham has existed within the depths of God from eternity; and the same is true of every sentient being. The simple intonation of Soham in time with the breath will do everything in the unfolding of the yogi's spiritual consciousness and will empower and transmute his entire being, including the subtle bodies that comprise his aura. Therefore it is the supreme psychic and spiritual defense. It is very important that you obtain and read the book, *Soham Yoga: The Yoga of the Self*, which gives the complete picture. Meanwhile here are the basic instructions on Soham Yoga Meditation.

The Practice of Soham Yoga Meditation

1) Sit upright, comfortable and relaxed, with your hands on your knees or thighs or resting, one on the other, in your lap.

2) Turn your eyes slightly downward and close them gently. This removes visual distractions and reduces your brain-wave activity by about seventy-five percent, thus helping to calm the mind. During meditation your eyes may move upward and downward naturally of their own accord. This is as it should be when it happens spontaneously. But start out with them turned slightly downward without any strain.

3) Be aware of your breath naturally (automatically) flowing in and out. Your mouth should be closed so that all breathing is done through the nose. This also aids in quieting the mind. Though your mouth is closed, the jaw muscles should be relaxed so the upper and lower teeth are not clenched or touching one another, but parted. Breathe naturally, spontaneously. Your breathing should always be easeful and natural, not deliberate or artificial.

4) Then in a very quiet and gentle manner begin mentally intoning Soham in time with your breathing. (Remember: Soham is pronounced like our English words So and Hum.)

Intone *Soooooo*, prolonging a single intonation throughout each inhalation, and *Huuummm*, prolonging a single intonation throughout each exhalation, "singing" the syllables on a single note.

There is no need to pull or push the mind. Let your relaxed attention sink into and get absorbed in the mental sound of your inner intonings of Soham.

Fit the intonations to the breath—not the breath to the intonations. If the breath is short, then the intonation should be short. If the breath is long, then the intonation should be long. It does not matter if the inhalations and exhalations are not of equal length. Whatever is natural and spontaneous is what is right.

Your intonation of *Soooooo* should begin when your inhalation begins, and *Huuummm* should begin when your exhalation begins. In this way your intonations should be virtually continuous, that is:

SooooooHuuummmSooooooHuuummmSooooooHuuum-mmSooooooHuuummm.

Do not torture yourself about this—basically continuous is good enough.

5) For the rest of your meditation time keep on intoning Soham in time with your breath, calmly listening to the mental sound.

6) In Soham meditation we do not deliberately concentrate on any particular point of the body such as the third eye, as we want the subtle energies of Soham to be free to manifest themselves as is best at the moment. However, as you meditate you may become aware of one or more areas of your brain or body at different times. This is all right when such sensations come and go spontaneously, but keep centered on your into-nations of Soham in time with your breath.

7) In time your inner mental intonations of Soham may change to a more mellow or softer form, even to an inner whispering that is almost silent, but the syllables are always

fully present and effective. Your intonations may even become silent, like a soundless mouthing of Soham or just the thought or movement of Soham, yet you will still be intoning Soham in your intention. And of this be sure: Soham never ceases. Never. You may find that your intonations of Soham move back and forth from more objective to more subtle and back to more objective. Just intone in the manner that is natural at the moment.

8) In the same way you will find that your breath will also become more subtle and refined, and slow down. Sometimes the breath may not be perceived as movement of the lungs, but just as the subtle pranic energy movement which causes the physical breath. Your breath can even become so light that it seems as though you are not breathing at all, just thinking the breath (or almost so).

9) Thoughts, impressions, memories, inner sensations, and suchlike may also arise during meditation. Be calmly aware of all these things in a detached and objective manner, but keep your attention centered in your intonations of Soham in time with your breath. Do not let your attention become centered on or caught up in any inner or outer phenomena. Be calmly aware of all these things in a detached and objective manner. They are part of the transforming work of Soham, and are perfectly all right, but keep your attention centered in your intonations of Soham in time with your breath. Even though something feels very right or good when it occurs, it should not be forced or hung on to. The sum and substance of it all is this: It is not the experience we are after, but the

effect. Also, since we are all different, no one can say exactly what a person's experiences in meditation are going to be like.

10) Soham japa and meditation can make us aware of the subtle levels of our being, many of which are out of phase with one another and are either confused or reversed in their polarity. The japa and meditation correct these things, but sometimes, especially at the beginning of meditation, we can experience these aberrations as uncomfortable or uneasy sensations, a feeling or heaviness or stasis or other peculiar sensations that are generally uncomfortable and somehow feel "not right." When this occurs, do not try to interfere with it or "make it better." Rather, just relax, keep on with the japa/meditation, calmly aware and let it be as it is. In time the problem in the subtle energy levels will be corrected and the feeling will become easy and pleasant. Simple as the practice is, it has deep and far-reaching effects, as you will see for yourself.

11) If you find yourself getting restless, distracted, fuzzy, anxious or tense in any degree, just take a deep breath and let it out fully, feeling that you are releasing and breathing out all tensions, and continue as before.

12) Remember: Soham Yoga meditation basically consists of four things: a) sitting with the eyes closed; b) being aware of our breath as it moves in and out; c) mentally intoning Soham in time with the breath; and d) listening to those mental intonations: all in a relaxed and easeful manner, without strain.

Breath and sound are the two major spiritual powers possessed by us, so they are combined for Soham Yoga practice. It is very natural to intone Soham in time with the breathing.

13) At the end of your meditation time, keep on intoning Soham in time with your breath as you go about your various activities, listening to the inner mantric sound, just as in meditation. One of the cardinal virtues of Soham sadhana is its capacity to be practiced throughout the day. The *Yoga Rasyanam* in verse 303 says: "Before and after the regular [meditation] practice, the repetition of Soham should be continuously done [in time with the breath] while walking, sitting or even sleeping.... This leads to ultimate success." By intentionally intoning So and Ham with the breath we are linking the conscious with the superconscious mind, bringing the superconscious onto the conscious level and merging them until they become one.

Can it be that simple and easy? Yes, because it goes directly to the root of our bondage which is a single–and therefore simple–thing: loss of awareness. Soham is the seed (bija) mantra of nirvanic consciousness. You take a seed, put it in the soil, water it and the sun does the rest. You plant the seed of Soham in your inner consciousness through japa and meditation and both your Self and the Supreme Self do the rest. By intentionally intoning *So* and *Ham* with the breath we are linking the conscious with the superconscious mind, bringing the superconscious onto the conscious level and merging them until they become one. This is what the Bhagavad Gita (6:29) means by the term yoga-yukta–joined to yoga. It is divinely simple!

Again: obtain and read the book *Soham Yoga: The Yoga of the Self.*

CHAPTER FIVE

BLESSING AND DEFENSE THROUGH SOHAM THEURGY

"Theurgy" is a word rarely used. It is a Greek word meaning "Divine Work." It may be called religious or spiritual magic, since its application is totally an invocation of divine consciousness and power. Theurgy can involve many forms of invocation, but obviously Soham Theurgy is based on Soham as the ultimate Word of Power.

Let's begin. Remember: whenever I say "intone Soham" I mean mentally intone Soham in time with your natural, spontaneous breathing: *So* when you inhale and *Ham* when you exhale.

Filling a place with Soham vibrations

When you mentally intone Soham with your attention at the Sahasrara chakra, the brain, the light and power of Soham keeps on building up throughout your aura and expanding it as long as you keep on intoning Soham. Everyone and everything encompassed by that light and power will be uplifted and benefitted. In this way you can fill a room, an entire building or large outdoor area with the vibrations of Soham. In this way you can bless a limitless number of people wherever you go. Please do not neglect this simple but wondrous practice.

In the next chapter I will be telling you about the freeing of some earthbound spirits and an "outside" spirit trapped in the earth plane through the work of Marcel Vogel and myself. But here I want to tell you about another thing that occurred at the same time. After Marcel had freed the "outside" spirit we went through the second floor of the building easily freeing the earthbound spirits. Then we came to the ground floor. The pastor of the metaphysical church had told everyone who had offices or other quarters in the building to be sure and leave all doors unlocked so Marcel and I could go into each room in our investigation. We came to a room that was locked, although the New Age psychologist who used it had been told to leave it unlocked.

Marcel and I looked at one another. We understood the situation, because a truly negative and malicious energy radiated through the door. "Let's go in," said Marcel, so we psychically projected into the room. Immediately I said, "I see a great sphere of rainbow light, and it feels absolutely positive." "Yes it is," replied Marcel, "That is me! Let's get to work." We did and filled the room with sacred vibrations. The tangible negativity melted away and light pervaded everywhere. "Let's go out," said Marcel, and so we did. Marcel, who was a no-nonsense person, made sure that the pastor learned about the incident. But the pastor did not need to take any action. The next day when no one was around the psychologist came and took all his things from the room and was never heard from again. Sometimes humans need to be exorcised from a place along with negative energies and entities.

Sending Soham vibrations to an individual who is present

Simply look at a person (directly or indirectly) and silently intone Soham in time with your own breath, feeling or imagining the sound of Soham vibrating through them.

If they or others present will not be able to see you doing it, raise your right hand–cupped, not flat–with the palm turned toward them. Mentally intone Soham in time with your breath, aware of the vibrations of Soham flowing to them. Do this until you feel you have done enough.

Sending Soham vibrations to an individual who is not present

If you know where the person is at the time, turn in that direction. If you do not, then turn or face toward the north or just bring them to mind if you do not know where north is.

Sit or stand quietly, raise your cupped right hand and bring the person to mind. Then mentally intone Soham in time with your breath, feeling and intending that the Soham vibrations are reaching and pervading them. Continue until you feel you have done enough. Do this facing the general direction where they are. If you do not know the direction where they are, then do this turned to the north, holding the intention that the Soham vibrations are reaching them.

If others are with you, then simply fix your mind on the person and intone Soham with the intention that the vibrations are reaching them.

You can do the same thing in relation to a place in general, including a group of people.

Wherever you sense help is needed, turn in that direction (or north if you do not know the general direction), hold up your cupped right hand and intone Soham in time with your breath, intending it to reach the "target."

Blessing objects with Soham

Blessed objects are powerful defenses and empowerments. You bless objects by filling them with Soham vibrations. There are three ways to do this:

1) Turn your cupped right hand toward the object and intone Soham in time with your breath for five breaths: at the same time feeling/willing the Soham vibrations emanating from your hand to enter and permeate the object fully. Five intonations of Soham in time with the breath is sufficient: the first intonation locks the Soham vibrations in the object and the subsequent four intonations fill it up completely and permanently.

2) Hold or touch the object while looking at it intently as you do the five intonations of Soham while willing the vibrations to enter it.

3) Simply look at the object intently as you do the five intonations of Soham while willing the vibrations to enter it.

All food, drink and medicine—anything to be ingested—should be first filled with Soham in one of these ways.

Blessed Water, Salt and Oil

Blessed water, salt and oil are very helpful tools for purification, blessing and protection. You bless them in one of the manners just described. According to the circumstances, you might want to keep some water, salt and oil in your automobile or other vehicle and even to carry small containers in your pocket or purse.

Blessed Water

Use the blessed water to purify and elevate the vibrations of an object or place by sprinkling it with the water.

Drawing a line with water at the threshold of a room or house is a powerful protection against the incursion of negative entities or energies.

Drinking blessed water is an effective blessing, purification and protection.

If possible the water should be pure, natural water–not distilled or with added chemicals–unless there is nothing else at hand.

Blessed Salt

Use blessed salt to break negative psychic links and clear an object or place by lightly sprinkling it around. This is why in earlier centuries blessed salt was put on the tongue of those about to be baptized. Putting blessed salt in the food of someone who is obsessed or possessed can dislodge the evil entities or energies. I once saw a severely obsessed person freed in three days just by having blessed salt put in her food or water (without her knowing it, of course). A tiny pinch is enough.

It is good to cook with blessed salt.

The salt should be pure, natural salt–organic is preferred.

Blessed Oil

Blessed oil strengthens and heals. It should be put on a person's forehead and any place where there is pain or injury, etc.

Blessed oil with a pinch of blessed salt added is very good for shielding and expelling negative energies and influences. An object that seems to be negatively magnetized can be touched with it. Touch a bit to your forehead or any place where you feel there might be negative energies. You can even put a touch of the oil in the center of the sole of each foot, and in the palm of each hand as well as the forehead and the crown of the head. This is very helpful in time of psychic attack or when you are about to encounter some negativity.

The oil should be pure olive oil–organic if possible.

Incense

Bless sticks of incense with Soham, then light one or more of them while mentally intoning Soham in time with your breath. The incense smoke will radiate and impart the vibrations of Soham as long as the incense burns. This is very purifying and uplifting.

Stick incense that has been blessed is very effective in psychic defense, much like blessed candles. Genuine sandalwood incense is particularly effective, as sandalwood has extremely high vibrations. Stick incense made of powdered frankincense is also very good. Two of the best brands to use are Goloka or Auroshika, as the ingredients are genuine and pure.

Candles

Bless a candle with Soham. Light the wick of the candle mentally intoning Soham. The candle will radiate the blessing and purifying vibrations of Soham as long as it burns, blessing everything the light touches. You can also hold a specific intention or purpose in mind as you bless and light the candle.

Shielding yourself

To shield yourself from a psychic attack or negative vibrations in general you can light a blessed candle or incense, or put some blessed salt on your tongue, or drink some blessed water, or put some blessed oil on the center of your forehead (just a dot will do). Or do all of these things. If you are with someone who needs shielding, do the same for them.

CHAPTER SIX

PHYSICAL OBJECTS THAT PSYCHICALLY DEFEND

On a very deep level all objects are "thought forms." That is, they are embodiments of actual concepts, and since "thoughts are things" they are the objectification of ideas and mental-psychic intentions. They are like shields that protect by resisting, deflecting, or even dissolving negative vibrations, including thought and will (intention) vibrations.

Holy Imagery

Depictions, either two-dimensional or three-dimensional, of sacred objects or persons can be powerful defenses against negative vibrations or presences. It has long been known that a cross or a crucifix have great exorcistic power. Holy scriptures also carry sacred vibrations and their very presence can repel negative vibrations or consciousness.

But depictions of holy persons, angels or deities are virtual presences of those depicted by them. And if these depictions have been ritually blessed they are practically speaking the living, spiritual presence of those sacred beings.

Therefore the presence of sacred images, two- or three-dimensional, both invoke and convey the holy vibrations of those depicted by the images. They repel negative vibrations and negative consciousnesses such as negative spirits or astral beings and even physically embodied people that are negative in thought and deed. The reaction of someone to a sacred depiction can reveal a great deal about their fundamental spiritual state.

Most important, negative spirits are repelled by holy depictions and usually cannot endure being in the same place with them.

People that are obsessed or even possessed by evil spirits hate and are made miserable by the mere presence of holy imagery. So you can diagnose the inner condition a person by their reaction to–or seemingly complete ignoring of–a sacred depiction.

Ritual blessing of an object

As I have said, the ritual blessing of an object purifies and empowers it greatly. And you can do such a blessing yourself with the sacred mantra Soham. Here is how.

1) Slightly cup your right hand so it is like a parabolic mirror and turn it toward the object. This focuses the pranic current moving from your hand onto and into the object.

2) Looking intently at the object and being very aware of (feeling) your hand pointing toward it, silently inhale and then exhale while mentally intoning Soham and feeling that

the subtle, mental sound vibrations of Soham are flowing into and pervading that object.

3) Repeat the foregoing three more times so you will have for a total of four times imbued that object with the vibrations of Soham.

You can empower water with these three steps and drink it for your benefit or sprinkle whatever or wherever you wish the divine vibrations of Soham to pervade. Usually I drink only Soham water empowered in this way. That way it pervades my entire body, empowering and shielding it.

There are two objects that themselves have exorcistic, healing and energizing effects: rudraksha beads and Saint Benedict medals.

Saint Benedict Medal

The medal of Saint Benedict has a marvelous effect of shielding the wearer from negative vibrations both in himself physically and mentally, and in his environment, including the vibrations of the people around him. It is best if the medal is touching the skin. It also can be placed in an area where protection and shielding are desired.

I would like to tell you its history. First, it had nothing to do with Saint Benedict himself. It originated many, many centuries after Saint Benedict lived.

Second, its creation came about because of two factors or conditions.

The practice of witchcraft or negative magic was rife in Europe many centuries ago, and everyone was afraid of being cursed or "hexed" by witches or warlocks (male witches). Gypsies made a goodly bit of money by selling amulets for protection against such cursing or hexing, but it was commonly thought that they first themselves did the cursing and then removed it when paid for protection. (This is portrayed in the 1947 Hollywood movie *The Golden Earrings*.)

Whatever may have been the actual situation, it was noticed in rural areas that there were farms and households where there was never any kind of psychic disturbance or misfortune. In time it was discovered that somewhere in each one of these places there was pattern of letters in a cross form surrounded by other letters. Not words; just letters.

In one district there was a Benedictine monastery whose presence seemed to shield the nearby district from any psychic or magical disturbances. It was well known that witches and sorcerers could not function in that area. Believing that it was the monastery which prevented the presence of negative magic, it was thoroughly searched and in the attics under the eaves the same mysterious letters were found that were in the protected farmhouses. A search in the monastery library found an ancient document that gave the mystical letters as "The Cross Of Our Holy Father Saint Benedict." And the letters proved to be the initial letters of an exorcistic formula in Latin that was a rebuke of evil forces and a demand for their departure. And apparently it worked. So in time medals were made and found to possess powers of blessing and exorcism. A ritual was created for their blessing/empowerment and has been in use ever since. But only a priest can perform it.

However you can empower the medals yourself using the "Ritual blessing of an object" through Soham I have given just previously. They can be bought from Catholic stores or supply houses, and even on Amazon.

Rudraksha beads

Rudraksha ("Eye of Shiva") beads are very powerful spiritual presences wherever they are kept or worn. (Wearing them is the preferred and most beneficial use.) Genuine rudraksha beads are known from the vertical lines that divide them into sections or "faces." The five-faced beads are preferred by the yogis because they contain or embody a perfect blend of the five basic vibrations of relative existence and therefore both strengthen, stabilize and balance the vibrations of the wearer's physical and subtle bodies.

Five-faced rudraksha beads can be bought online for very reasonable prices. But beware of "rudraksha centers" and the "experts" that pedal various kinds of rudraksha for magical-type effects, especially financial prosperity–for a very high price. There is also traffic in faked beads of differing numbers of faces.

Five-faced rudraksha beads act like antennae that pull in beneficial vibrations and convey them to the body of the wearer. So they empower and stabilize the wearer. At the same time, rudraksha beads can pull in and absorb negative energies that enter the wearer's aura. Therefore they occasionally need to be cleared and freed of those vibrations. I only do it every few months, myself. The way to clear them is very easy. Turn on the cold water faucet and taking them in your hand, hold them under the water and let it very thoroughly wash over them to carry away the subtle energies they have absorbed. This does not take a long time.

The beads can become dried both from time and from perspiration and various bodily elements touching them. So after clearing them with water it is good to take a small amount of ghee (clarified butter) such as you can get in grocery stores (especially Indian ones) or even regular stores. (Costco sells ghee in glass jars.) Rub the ghee over all the beads. One way is to put the ghee in the palm of one hand and rub the beads between both your hands in a circular motion. Anandamayi Ma used to bless rudrakshas by this way of rubbing them between her palms.

Rudrakshas have a very real innate power, but you can bless/empower them with the "Ritual blessing of an object" through Soham if you like.

CHAPTER SEVEN

OBSESSION AND POSSESSION BY SPIRITS

There are such things as negative spirits. Some are earth-bound human beings and some are non-human spirits of the earth or spirits that have wandered into our dimension from other universes. Others were involved in the creation of our universe, yet somehow fell into the ways of folly and negativity. Therefore some are malevolent and others are not. Many are frightened and confused.

Obsession is influence by a spirit, and possession is domination and control by a spirit. More on that soon.

I have had a goodly bit of experience with spirits, and it is not at all uncommon for people to encounter them, but they often do not know what they are faced with. Sometimes both the human and the spirit frighten each other!

Never believe the threats of spirits. It is all noise and bluff. But never laugh, mock or speak with anger, contempt or hatred to them, because that can empower them. And besides, it is wrong to do because they are God's children also. Just be calm and refuse to be affected by them.

On occasion simply ignoring them can make them leave because it unsettles their ego and frustrates them.

Sometimes I have gotten rid of a possibly negative spirit simply by saying: "If you don't go away I will bless you," or: "If you don't go away I will pray to God that he will give you his love and deliver you from your evil." Neither of these appeal to truly evil spirits.

Negative and foolish entities can oppress and harm human beings in various ways, but the worst are obsession and possession by such spirits.

Obsession

Obsession by a spirit occurs when a spirit lodges itself in the aura of a someone or enters into his body–usually only partially. That is, the entity does not pervade the victim's entire body, mind and personality. Often obsessed people think they are only ill in some manner, or that they ache or hurt for some physical reason.

In obsession there is usually no outright control of the person or of his mind, but rather distraction and confusion. He feels mentally foggy or senses that "something is not just right," but has no idea what. He may consult a physician and be told he is perfectly all right, and therefore he worries that something is wrong with him mentally or that he is just imagining there is a problem.

In obsession the victim is influenced, but not completely controlled as in possession. However, obsessing spirits often insinuate negative ideas or impulses into the obsessed person's

mind and body–even addictions. Smoking tobacco or mari-
juana, etc., and drinking alcohol can attract spirits and make
us susceptible to their influence.

Obsession in varying degrees is all around us. And it
often comes and goes erratically. Yogis may have obsessed
people react to them in a very marked way. Obsessed persons
may become hostile to them on sight and be very rude or
insulting in conversations with other people around. One
yogi wrote to me that after he began Soham sadhana some
people on the street would make faces at him at first sight,
and others would turn around and run away as through
terrified at seeing him.

One sign of obsession is a person's reluctance or refusal
to enter a holy place or a yogi's house. Somehow they just
no longer find the time for a visit since you became a yogi.
Through the years we have experienced people being unable
to even walk onto our ashram property.

Some years ago I gave talks on the Bhagavad Gita on Friday
evenings at our ashram. Above the main ashram door I put a
picture of Ganesha, who guards and protects. When I put up
the picture I looked at him and said, "Ganapati, please do not
let anyone in this door that you don't like." A short time later
I transcribed some exorcistic protection mantras and attached
them to the back of the picture. A few weeks later a car drove
up on a Friday evening and four people got out and came up
the walk to the ashram. Three of them came right in, but the
fourth just stood outside, seeming to be pushing against an
invisible barrier. "Come on in!" urged the three, but the man

seemingly could not do it. Suddenly he turned around and ran to the car, jumped in and roared off, leaving the others stranded. Later we learned that this man was involved in some very negative occult practices.

A great deal of mental and physical suffering, imbalance and upset can result from obsession, but it is very slight compared with possession.

Possession

Possession occurs when a spirit enters and completely controls someone—literally begins living through the victim's body. Often the subtle body of the victim is pushed right out of his body into his aura, the field of bio-energies surrounding it. So he is outside his body observing the possessing spirit's total control. This is a terrifying and mind-bending experience.

On rare occasions the possessing entity completely and permanently breaks the possessed person's connections with the body.

Interestingly, the possessed person's pulse may reveal one of two conditions. In ordinary possession the victim's heart may keep skipping a beat in a steady pattern of an exact number of normal beats before one beat fails to occur. But when the victim has been completely expelled from his body and only the possessing spirit remains, he is for all practical purposes "dead," and there is no heartbeat at all, but rather a kind of heavy electrical "current" or heavy pulsation moving through the heart and veins.

Serious advice!

Do not attempt exorcism of a possessed person, or of one only suspected of being possessed, in the presence of that person. Do everything from a distance. This is crucial, for the possessing entity often physically attacks those trying to exorcise it. Also a possessing entity often threatens that it will kill the possessed person if there is an attempt to exorcise him.

Both exorcism from a distance and in the presence of the possessed person is written about in the Bible: "God wrought special miracles by the hands of Paul: so that from his body were brought unto the sick handkerchiefs or aprons, and the diseases departed from them, and the evil spirits went out of them. Then certain of the vagabond Jews, exorcists, took upon them to call over them which had evil spirits the name of the Lord Jesus, saying, We adjure you by Jesus whom Paul preacheth. And there were seven sons of one Sceva, a Jew, and chief of the priests, which did so. And the evil spirit answered and said, Jesus I know, and Paul I know; but who are ye? And the man in whom the evil spirit was leaped on them, and overcame them, and prevailed against them, so that they fled out of that house naked and wounded" (Acts 19:11-16).

Here we see two means of exorcism: from a distance and in person. And we see the results of the exorcism being attempted in person. So do not attempt in-person exorcism unless you are suddenly confronted with a possessed person. Even then, do nothing overt in relation to the possessed one, but work unobserved.

If possible, see if salt blessed with Soham can be put in the person's food or water blessed with Soham be given to them to drink. That may be sufficient and you will not need to do anything else. You need not should not be present at this–others can do it.

If possible, have blessed incense or a blessed candle lit where the person is. But if there is an intensely negative or violent reaction they should be immediately extinguished.

And further...

Some psychotic people pretend to be possessed so they can gain attention and mess with the minds of those around them. Get them to leave or leave yourself. They are beyond help because they do not want help.

Soham Theurgy At A Distance For Obsession and Possession

1) Sit for Soham Meditation for some time to fill yourself and the place you are in with the vibrations of Soham.

2) Sitting or standing, turn in the general direction of the person to be helped. Raise your cupped right hand and bring the afflicted person to mind. Then mentally intone Soham, feeling and intending that the vibrations are reaching and pervading them. Continue until you feel you have done enough. Do this facing the general direction where they are, but if you do not know the direction where they are, then do this turned to the north, holding the intention that the Soham vibrations are reaching them.

You can do steps 1 & 2 more than once, according to your intuition or perceived need.

As much as is practical, keep your attention at the Sahasrara chakra during this process. (This is not absolutely necessary, but can be a definite help in obtaining the needed effect.)

If no results are obtained, you can repeat everything, but use your intuition as to when you should stop and leave it alone. Also, whether you suspect obsession or possession, be aware that it may just be a case of negativity on the part of a negative person.

Also be aware that some people either consciously or subconsciously do not want to be free of the spirit that is obsessing or possessing them. If this proves to be the case, then stop your efforts, for the victim is choosing his condition by his own free will.

It is also a good idea before formal working to put some blessed salt on your tongue, or drink some blessed water, or put some blessed oil on the center of your forehead (just a dot will do).

I recommend that you usually never do any work in the actual presence of the obsessed or possessed person needing help (you could do it in the same building, but not in their presence). However, if you feel there is an exception to this rule, act accordingly.

Why would yogis encounter evil or earthbound, wandering spirits?

Because it is the karma of both: his to exorcise and theirs to be exorcised.

Always remember that the positive expels the negative. Therefore blessing is usually the best form of exorcism. I have seen possessed and obsessed people freed quickly and easily (and without drama) by such means.

On occasion I have found that praying for an entity can benefit it. This is because some spirits actually come for help, but at the same time their deep negativity may impel them to be hostile and threatening–they cannot help themselves. On the other hand, do not let spirits fool you by pretending they need you to keep on "helping" them by praying and suchlike. This is just a way to tie you to them. If something does not get rid of them right away, then another approach is needed.

One of Swami Sivananda's disciples told me that in an Indian scripture it is written that once many evil spirits came to Brahma the Creator and asked how they could be delivered from their negative condition, for their evil rendered them unable to help themselves. Brahma told them to seek out true yogis and sadhakas and stay near them and in time they would be freed. In India I have been in some ashrams and holy places that were incredibly haunted by such spirits. I once read an account by a Westerner who had encountered negative spirits in one of the holiest shrines of Shiva, who is merciful to evil and crazy spirits.

I know of another yogi who began seeing a terrifying and threatening entity every time he sat for meditation. He determinedly ignored it and forced himself to keep sitting and meditating. After about four times the thing no longer appeared.

As I have said, the yogi may have such experiences because of some previous life karma. Usually, though, the japa and meditation of Soham draw that which is good and repel that which is evil. If evil in the form of entities or energies approaches and japa and meditation are maintained calmly by the yogi, then it right away or eventually leaves, dissolves or is transmuted.

As I have said, spirits come to us for help. Even though many spirits spend their time harming and terrifying people because of their hatred and malice, some really do want to be freed from their miserable state, even though because of their addiction to evil they still manifest hostility toward the people or place from which they seek help. They cannot help themselves, just as humans with evil habits both want to rid themselves of their addictions and at the same time want to hold on to them.

Always remember: the core of all evil spirits is the same divine spirit-self that is at the core of all beings. That is why they can be freed.

Those who see a demon behind every bush or grain of sand will say: "Aha! You are telling people to sympathize with evil spirits and in that way get under their power!" There is no doubt that a foolish and sentimental sympathy will not help those spirits, and they can start pestering and even tormenting those that do not try to help them in the right way. And in fact, there are times when they must kindly be told:

"I cannot help you. Please go elsewhere." I have had to do so myself on occasion, because otherwise the incautious yogi can become swamped by such spirits. Knowing our limitations and acting accordingly is an important asset in many aspects of life, including this.

If the spirit does not go, then japa and meditation of Soham, sprinkling of water blessed by Soham and fire (candles) blessed by Soham as I described earlier must come into use.

Be cautious, but fear not.

Animal spirits

Animal spirits can be earthbound, too. Since they do not have human intelligence you cannot talk to them, but you can pray for them and even ask their guardian spirits (they have them) to come help them or to ask holy angels to come to their aid.

A final word

Avoid those who are obsessed with evil and the Devil, demons and black magicians, etc., and keep company with those who are devoted to God and his holy ones.

Though thousands of words have been produced on the subject of psychic defense, in the final summation it will be seen that the secret of psychic defense is simply strength within one's own spirit-self. If our physical, psychic and spiritual levels are all strongly vibrating with higher consciousness, the "whole armor of God" (Ephesians 6:11-13), then we are effortlessly invincible. The motto "God is my strength," is no poetic fancy, but bedrock fact. So our real defense is good spiritual health.

The best psychic defense is to keep up the level of your personal energies. If you do so, many onslaughts of negativity will be so effortlessly and automatically turned back that you will not even be aware of them.

In time of negative bombardment, the correct method of defense is to put your mind fully on God. For the essence of defense is strength of personal vibration. When your aura is strong with the Divine Light, no evil thing can penetrate it. Therefore the constant japa and meditation of Soham are the highest defenses. Again, I strongly recommend that you obtain and read the book, *Soham Yoga: The Yoga of the Self.*

In my younger years I used to sing in church a hymn whose refrain about the spiritually wise is still relevant:

> That wicked one toucheth him not,
> That wicked one toucheth him not;
> He keepeth himself in the love of the Lord,
> And that wicked one toucheth him not.

DID YOU ENJOY
READING THIS BOOK?

Thank you for taking the time to read *Psychic Defense for Yogis*. If you found it meaningful, or if it inspired you, or simply gave you something worth pondering, we invite you to leave a short review on Amazon, Goodreads, or anywhere books are shared.

Word of mouth is one of the greatest gifts you can offer to independent publishers, and helps keep this work in motion.

CONTINUE Your Journey Within:
GET YOUR FREE
MEDITATION GUIDE

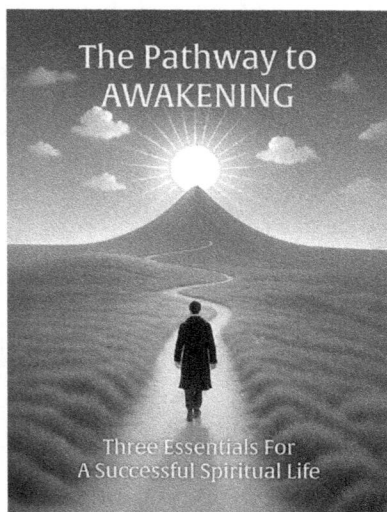

Sign up for the Light of the Spirit Newsletter and get
The Pathway to Awakening: Three Essentials for a Successful Spiritual Life

Get free updates: newsletters, blog posts, and podcasts, plus exclusive content from Light of the Spirit Monastery.

Visit: https://ocoy.org/signup

ABOUT THE AUTHOR

Swami Nirmalananda Giri (**Abbot George Burke**) is the founder and director of the Atma Jyoti Ashram (Light of the Spirit Monastery) in Cedar Crest, New Mexico, USA.

In his many pilgrimages to India, he had the opportunity of meeting some of India's greatest spiritual figures, including Swami Sivananda of Rishikesh and Anandamayi Ma. During his first trip to India he was made a member of the ancient Swami Order by Swami Vidyananda Giri, a direct disciple of Paramhansa Yogananda, who had himself been given sannyas by the Shankaracharya of Puri, Jagadguru Bharati Krishna Tirtha.

In the United States he also encountered various Christian saints, including Saint John Maximovich of San Francisco and Saint Philaret Voznesensky of New York.

For many years Swami Nirmalananda has researched the identity of Jesus Christ and his teachings with India and Sanatana Dharma, including Yoga. It is his conclusion that Jesus lived in India for most of his life, and was a yogi and Sanatana Dharma missionary to the West. After his resurrection he returned to India and lived the rest of his life in the Himalayas.

He has written extensively on these and other topics, many of which are posted at OCOY.org.

ATMA JYOTI ASHRAM
(LIGHT OF THE SPIRIT MONASTERY)

Atma Jyoti Ashram (Light of the Spirit Monastery) is a monastic community for those men who seek direct experience of the Spirit through yoga meditation, traditional yogic discipline, Sanatana Dharma and the life of the sannyasi in the tradition of the Order of Shankara. Our lineage is in the Giri branch of the Order.

The public outreach of the monastery is through its website, OCOY.org (Original Christianity and Original Yoga). There you will find many articles on Original Christianity and Original Yoga, including *The Christ of India*. *Foundations of Yoga* and *How to Be a Yogi* are practical guides for anyone seriously interested in living the Yoga Life.

You will also discover many other articles on leading an effective spiritual life, including *Soham Yoga: The Yoga of the Self* and *Spiritual Benefits of a Vegetarian Diet*, as well as the "Dharma for Awakening" series—in-depth commentaries on these spiritual classics: the Bhagavad Gita, the Upanishads, the Dhammapada, the Tao Teh King and more.

You can listen to podcasts by Swami Nirmalananda on meditation, the Yoga Life, and remarkable spiritual people he has met in India and elsewhere, at http://ocoy.org/podcasts/

Join over 33,000 subscribers and watch over 300 videos on these topics and more, including recordings of online satsangs where Swami Nirmalananda answers various questions on practical aspects of spiritual life. A new series of talks on the Bhagavad Gita has also been added.

Visit our Youtube channel here:
Youtube.com/@lightofthespirit

READING FOR AWAKENING

Light of the Spirit Press presents books on spiritual wisdom and Original Christianity and Original Yoga. From our "Dharma for Awakening" series (practical commentaries on the world's scriptures) to books on how to meditate and live a successful spiritual life, you will find books that are informative, helpful, and even entertaining.

Light of the Spirit Press is the publishing house of Light of the Spirit Monastery (Atma Jyoti Ashram) in Cedar Crest, New Mexico, USA. Our books feature the writings of the founder and director of the monastery, Swami Nirmalananda Giri (Abbot George Burke) which are also found on the monastery's website, OCOY.org.

We invite you to explore our publications in the following pages.

Find out more about our publications at
lightofthespiritpress.com

BOOKS ON MEDITATION

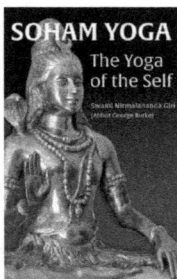

Soham Yoga
The Yoga of the Self

A complete and in-depth guide to effective meditation and the life that supports it, this important book explains with clarity and insight what real yoga is, and why and how to practice Soham Yoga meditation.

Discovered centuries ago by the Nath yogis, this simple and classic approach to self-realization has no "secrets," requires no "initiation," and is easily accessible to the serious modern yogi.

Includes helpful, practical advice on leading an effective spiritual life and many Illuminating quotes on Soham from Indian scriptures and great yogis.

"This book is a complete spiritual path." –Arnold Van Wie

Light of Soham
The Life and Teachings of Sri Gajanana Maharaj of Nashik

Gajanan Murlidhar Gupte, later known as Gajanana Maharaj, led an unassuming life, to all appearances a normal unmarried man of contemporary society. Crediting his personal transformation to the practice of the Soham mantra, he freely shared this practice with a small number of disciples, whom he simply called his friends. Strictly avoiding the trap of gurudom, he insisted that his friends be self-reliant and not be dependent on him for their spiritual progress. Yet he was uniquely able to assist them in their inner development.

The Inspired Wisdom of Gajanana Maharaj
A Practical Commentary on Leading an Effectual Spiritual Life

Presents the teachings and sayings of the great twentieth-century Soham yogi Gajanana Maharaj, with a commentary by Swami Nirmalananda.

The author writes: "In reading about Gajanana Maharaj I encountered a holy personality that eclipsed all others for me. In his words I found a unique wisdom that altered my perspective on what yoga, yogis, and gurus should be.

"But I realized that through no fault of their own, many Western readers need a clarification and expansion of Maharaj's meaning to get the right understanding of his words. This commentary is meant to help my friends who, like me have found his words 'a light in the darkness.'"

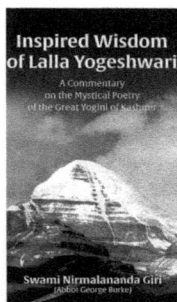

Inspired Wisdom of Lalla Yogeshwari
A Commentary on the Mystical Poetry of the Great Yogini of Kashmir

Lalla Yogeshwari was a great fourteenth-century yogini and wandering ascetic of Kashmir, whose mystic poetry were the earliest compositions in the Kashmiri language. She was in the tradition of the Nath Yogi Sampradaya whose meditation practice is that of Soham Sadhana: the joining of the mental repetition of Soham Mantra with the natural breath.

Swami Nirmalananda's commentary mines the treasures of Lalleshwari's mystic poems and presents his reflections in an easily intelligible fashion for those wishing to put these priceless teachings on the path of yogic self-transformation into practice.

Dwelling in the Mirror
A Study of Illusions Produced By Delusive Meditation
And How to Be Free from Them

Swami Nirmalananda says of this book: "There are those who can have an experience and realize that it really cannot be real, but a vagary of their mind. Some may not understand that on their own, but can be shown by others the truth about it. For them and those that may one day be in danger of meditation-produced delusions I have written this brief study."

BOOKS ON YOGA & SPIRITUAL LIFE

An Eagle's Flight
A Yogi's Spiritual Autobiography

Swami Nirmalananda Giri shares with rare honesty the struggles, insights, and blessings that have shaped his spiritual life.

Written with his usual insight, vividness, and humor, this book presents stories of his encounters with Anandamayi Ma, Swami Sivananda of Rishikesh and many other saints and yogis. This book offers inspiration, guidance, and a glimpse of what it means to live as a yogi in the modern world.

Satsang with the Abbot
Questions and Answers about Life, Spiritual Liberty,
and the Pursuit of Ultimate Happiness

The questions in this book range from the most sublime to the most practical. "How can I attain samadhi?" "I am married with children. How can I lead a spiritual life?" "What is Self-realization?" "How important is belief in karma and reincarnation?"

In Swami Nirmalananda's replies to these questions the reader will discover common sense, helpful information, and a guiding light for their journey through and beyond the forest of cliches, contradictions, and confusion of yoga, Hinduism, Christianity, and metaphysical thought.

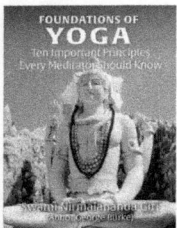

Foundations of Yoga
Ten Important Principles Every Meditator Should Know

An introduction to the important foundation principles of Patanjali's Yoga: Yama and Niyama

Yama and Niyama are often called the Ten Commandments of Yoga, but they have nothing to do with the ideas of sin and virtue or good and evil as dictated by some cosmic potentate. Rather they are determined by a thoroughly practical, pragmatic basis: that which strengthens and facilitates our yoga practice should be observed and that which weakens or hinders it should be avoided.

Yoga: Science of the Absolute
A Commentary on the Yoga Sutras of Patanjali

The Yoga Sutras of Patanjali is the most authoritative text on Yoga as a practice. It is also known as the Yoga Darshana because it is the fundamental text of Yoga as a philosophy.

In this commentary, Swami Nirmalananda draws on the age-long tradition regarding this essential text, including the commentaries of Vyasa and Shankara, the most highly regarded writers on Indian philosophy and practice, as well as I. K. Taimni and other authoritative commentators, and adds his own ideas based on half a century of study and practice. Serious students of yoga will find this an essential addition to their spiritual studies.

The Benefits of Brahmacharya

A Collection of Writings About the Spiritual,
Mental, and Physical Benefits of Continence

"Brahmacharya is the basis for morality. It is the basis for eternal life. It is a spring flower that exhales immortality from its petals." Swami Sivananda

This collection of articles from a variety of authorities including Mahatma Gandhi, Sri Ramakrishna, Swami Vivekananda, Swamis Sivananda and Chidananda of the Divine Life Society, Swami Nirmalananda, and medical experts, presents many facets of brahmacharya and will prove of immense value to all who wish to grow spiritually.

Living the Yoga Life

Perspectives on Yoga

"Dive deep; otherwise you cannot get the gems at the bottom of the ocean. You cannot pick up the gems if you only float on the surface." Sri Ramakrishna

In *Living the Yoga Life* Swami Nirmalananda shares the gems he has found from a lifetime of "diving deep." This collection of reflections and short essays addresses the key concepts of yoga philosophy that are so easy to take for granted. Never content with the accepted cliches about yoga sadhana, the yoga life, the place of a guru, the nature of Brahman and our unity with It, Swami Nirmalananda's insights on these and other facets of the yoga life will inspire, provoke, enlighten, and even entertain.

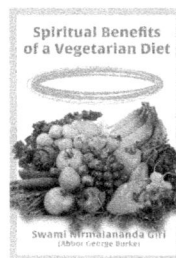

Spiritual Benefits of a Vegetarian Diet

The health benefits of a vegetarian diet are well known, as are the ethical aspects. But the spiritual advantages should be studied by anyone involved in meditation, yoga, or any type of spiritual practice.

Diet is a crucial aspect of emotional, intellectual, and spiritual development as well. For diet and consciousness are interrelated, and purity of diet is an effective aid to purity and clarity of consciousness.

The major thing to keep in mind when considering the subject of vegetarianism is its relevancy in relation to our explorations of consciousness. We need only ask: Does it facilitate my spiritual growth–the development and expansion of my consciousness? The answer is Yes.

BOOKS ON THE SACRED SCRIPTURES OF INDIA

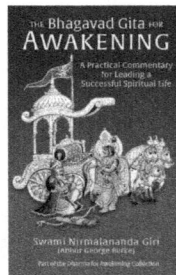

The Bhagavad Gita for Awakening

A Practical Commentary for Leading a Successful Spiritual Life

Drawing from the teachings of Sri Ramakrishna, Jesus, Paramhansa Yogananda, Ramana Maharshi, Swami Vivekananda, Swami Sivananda of Rishikesh, Papa Ramdas, and other spiritual masters and teachers, as well as his own experiences, Swami Nirmalananda illustrates the teachings of the Gita with stories which make the teachings of Krishna in the Gita vibrant and living.

From *Publisher's Weekly*: "[The author] enthusiastically explores the story as a means for knowing oneself, the cosmos, and one's calling within it. His plainspoken insights often distill complex lessons with simplicity and sagacity. Those with a deep interest in the Gita will find much wisdom here."

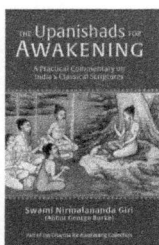

The Upanishads for Awakening
A Practical Commentary on India's Classical Scriptures

The sacred scriptures of India are vast. Yet they are only different ways of seeing the same thing, the One Thing which makes them both valid and ultimately harmonious. That unifying subject is Brahman: God the Absolute, beyond and besides whom there is no "other" whatsoever. The thirteen major Upanishads are the fountainhead of all expositions of Brahman.

Swamiji illumines the Upanishads' value for spiritual seekers from the unique perspective of a lifetime of study and practice of both Eastern and Western spirituality.

The Bhagavad Gita–The Song of God

Often called the "Bible" of Hinduism, the Bhagavad Gita is found in households throughout India and has been translated into every major language of the world. Literally billions of copies have been handwritten or printed.

The clarity of this translation by Swami Nirmalananda makes for easy reading, while the rich content makes this the ideal "study" Gita. As the original Sanskrit language is so rich, often there are several accurate translations for the same word, which are noted in the text, giving the spiritual student the needed understanding of the fullness of the Gita.

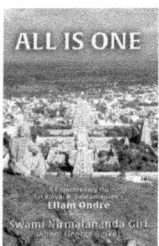

All Is One
A Commentary On Sri Vaiyai R. Subramanian's Ellam Ondre

Swami Nirmalananda's insightful commentary brings even further light to Ellam Ondre's refreshing perspective on what Unity signifies, and the path to its realization.

Written in the colorful and well-informed style typical of his other commentaries, it is a timely and important contribution to Advaitic literature that explains Unity as the fruit of yoga sadhana, rather than mere wishful thinking or some vague intellectual gymnastic, as is so commonly taught by the modern "Advaita gurus."

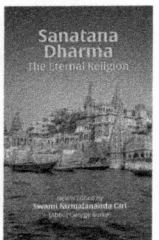

Sanatana Dharma
The Eternal Religion

Sanatana Dharma, commonly called Hinduism, is not just beautiful temples, colorful festivals, gurus and unusual beliefs. It is, simply put, "The Way Things Are" on a cosmic scale. It is the facts of existence and transcendence.

Swami Nirmalananda has edited for the modern reader a book originally printed nearly one hundred years ago in Varanasi, India, for use as a textbook by students of Benares Hindu University. Its original title was *Sanatana Dharma, An Advanced Text Book of Hindu Religion and Ethics*.

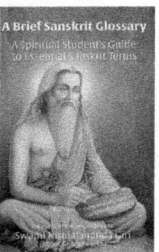

A Brief Sanskrit Glossary
A Spiritual Student's Guide to Essential Sanskrit Terms

This Sanskrit glossary contains full translations and explanations of hundreds of the most commonly used spiritual Sanskrit terms, and will help students of the Bhagavad Gita, the Upanishads, the Yoga Sutras of Patanjali, and other Indian scriptures and philosophical works to expand their vocabularies to include the Sanskrit terms contained in these, and gain a fuller understanding in their studies.

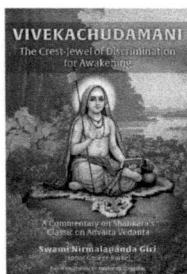

Vivekachudamani The Crest-Jewel of Discrimination For Awakening
A Commentary on Shankara's Classic on Advaita Vedanta

Beyond theory, this commentary offers practical insights for those seeking true spiritual growth, making it an essential guide for both beginners and advanced practitioners of Vedanta.

Whether you are a seasoned yogi or new to the path of spiritual awakening, this book will illuminate your journey, helping you discern the path to higher awareness amidst the clutter of modern spiritual clichés.

Dive into this classic text reimagined for contemporary seekers and transform your understanding of self and reality.

BOOKS ON ORIGINAL CHRISTIANITY

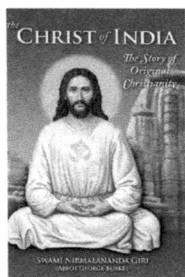

The Christ of India
The Story of Original Christianity

"Original Christianity" is the teaching of both Jesus and his Apostle Saint Thomas in India. Although it was new to the Mediterranean world, it was really the classical, traditional teachings of the rishis of India that even today comprise the Eternal Dharma, that goes far beyond religion into realization.

In *The Christ of India* Swami Nirmalananda presents what those ancient teachings are, as well as the growing evidence that Jesus spent much of his "Lost Years" in India and Tibet. This is also the story of how the original teachings of Jesus and Saint Thomas thrived in India for centuries before the coming of the European colonialists.

May a Christian Believe in Reincarnation?

Discover the real and surprising history of reincarnation and Christianity.

A growing number of people are open to the subject of past lives, and the belief in rebirth—reincarnation, metempsychosis, or transmigration—is commonplace. It often thought that belief in reincarnation and Christianity are incompatible. But is this really true? May a Christian believe in reincarnation? The answer may surprise you.

"Those needing evidence that a belief in reincarnation is in accordance with teachings of the Christ need look no further: Plainly laid out and explained in an intelligent manner from one who has spent his life on a Christ-like path of renunciation and prayer/meditation."—Christopher T. Cook

The Unknown Lives of Jesus and Mary
Compiled from Ancient Records and Mystical Revelations

"There are also many other things which Jesus did, the which, if they should be written every one, I suppose that even the world itself could not contain the books that should be written." (Gospel of Saint John, final verse)

You can discover much of those "many other things" in this unique compilation of ancient records and mystical revelations, which includes historical records of the lives of Jesus Christ and his Mother Mary that have been accepted and used by the Church since apostolic times. This treasury of little-known stories of Jesus' life will broaden the reader's understanding of what Christianity really was in its original form.

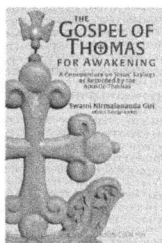

The Gospel of Thomas for Awakening
A Commentary on Jesus' Sayings as Recorded by the Apostle Thomas

When the Apostles dispersed to the various area of the world, Thomas travelled to India, where evidence shows Jesus spent his Lost Years, and which had been the source of the wisdom which he had brought to the "West."

The Christ that Saint Thomas quotes in this ancient text is quite different than the Christ presented by popular Christianity. Through his unique experience and study with both Christianity and Indian religion, Swami Nirmalananda clarifies the sometimes enigmatic sayings of Jesus in an informative and inspiring way.

The Odes of Solomon for Awakening
A Commentary on the Mystical Wisdom of the Earliest Christian Hymns and Poems

The Odes of Solomon is the earliest Christian hymn-book, and therefore one of the most important early Christian documents. Since they are mystical and esoteric, they teach and express the classical and universal mystical truths of Christianity, revealing a Christian perspective quite different than that of "Churchianity," and present the path of Christhood that all Christians are called to.

"I deeply appreciate Abbot George Burke's useful and illuminating insight and find myself spiritually re-animated." –John Lawhn

The Aquarian Gospel for Awakening (2 Volumes)
A Practical Commentary on Levi Dowling's Classic Life of Jesus Christ

Written in 1908 by the American mystic Levi Dowling, The Aquarian Gospel of Jesus the Christ answers many questions about Jesus' life that the Bible doesn't address. Dowling presents a universal message found at the heart of all valid religions, a broad vision of love and wisdom that will ring true with Christians who are attracted to Christ but put off by the narrow views of the tradition that has been given his name.

Swami Nirmalananda's commentary is a treasure-house of knowledge and insight.

Wandering With The Cherubim
A Commentary on the Mystical Verse of Angelus Silesius–The Cherubinic Wanderer"

Johannes Scheffler, who wrote under the name Angelus Silesius, was a mystic and a poet. In his most famous book, "The Cherubinic Wanderer," he expressed his mystical vision.

Swami Nirmalananda reveals the timelessness of his mystical teachings and The Cherubinic Wanderer's practical value for spiritual seekers. He does this in an easily intelligible fashion for those wishing to put those priceless teachings into practice.

"Set yourself on the journey of this mystical poetry made accessible through this very beautifully commentated text. It is text that submerges one in the philosophical context of the Advaita notion of Non Duality." –Savitri

Robe of Light
An Esoteric Christian Cosmology

In *Robe of Light* Swami Nirmalananda explores the whys and wherefores of the mystery of creation. From the emanation of the worlds from the very Being of God, to the evolution of the souls to their ultimate destiny as perfected Sons of God, the ideal progression of creation is described. Since the rebellion of Lucifer and the fall of Adam and Eve from Paradise flawed the normal plan of evolution, a restoration was necessary. How this came about is the prime subject of this insightful study.

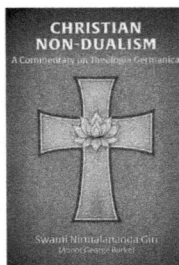

Christian Non-Dualism
A Commentary on Theologia Germanica

What if the roots of Christian mysticism held teachings as profound as those found in the East? What if a single medieval text, long forgotten by mainstream theology, offered a clear and proven path to inner union with God?

Christian Non-Dualism is a revelatory commentary on *Theologia Germanica*, a 14th-century mystical masterpiece that has gone through nearly 200 editions but is almost unknown today. With depth, clarity, and spiritual authority, Swami Nirmalananda Giri unveils the text's rich insights into ego-surrender, divine grace, and the path to inner revelation.

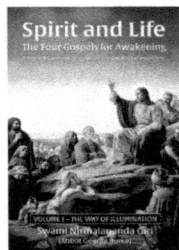

Spirit & Life–The Four Gospels for Awakening
A Practical Commentary on the Life and Teachings of Jesus Christ

Spirit & Life offers a powerful, practical commentary on a harmony of the Gospels, and is not a mere biography but a spiritual revelation consisting of both the life and the teachings of Jesus.

Far from being a conventional or doctrinal study, this book invites readers into the inner life of the soul, where Jesus is not only the Master Teacher, but the awakened Self within. With clarity and reverence, the author examines the inner meaning of the canonical Gospels, unveiling their universal message of illumination, liberation, and union with God.

A two volume set, beautifully illustrated.

BOOKS ON BUDDHISM & TAOISM AND MORE

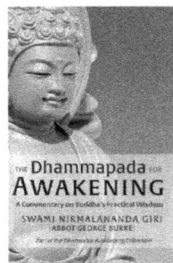

The Dhammapada for Awakening
A Commentary on Buddha's Practical Wisdom

Swami Nirmalananda's commentary on this classic Buddhist scripture explores the Buddha's answers to the urgent questions, such as "How can I find find lasting peace, happiness and fulfillment that seems so elusive?" and "What can I do to avoid many of the miseries big and small that afflict all of us?" Drawing on his personal experience, the author sheds new light on the Buddha's eternal wisdom.

"Swami Nirmalananda's commentary is well crafted and stacked with anecdotes, humor, literary references and beautiful quotes from the Buddha. I have come to consider it a guide to daily living." –Rev. Gerry Nangle

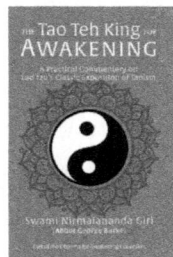

The Tao Teh King for Awakening
A Practical Commentary on Lao Tzu's Classic Exposition of Taoism

"The Tao does all things, yet our interior disposition determines our success or failure in coming to knowledge of the unknowable Tao."

Lao Tzu's classic writing, the Tao Teh King, has fascinated scholars and seekers for centuries. Swami Nirmalananda offers a commentary that makes the treasures of Lao Tzu's teachings accessible and applicable for the sincere seeker.

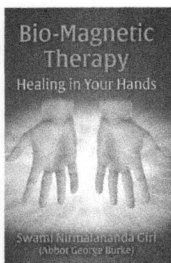

Bio-Magnetic Therapy
Healing in Your Hands

In *Bio-Magnetic Therapy* Swami Nirmalananda teaches the techniques to strengthen your vitality and improve the body's natural healing ability in yourself and in others with specific methods that anyone can use.

Bio-Magnetic Therapy is a simple and natural way to increase the flow of life-force into the body for general good health and to stimulate the supply and flow of life-force to a troubled area that has become vitality-starved through some obstruction. It does not cure; it simply aids the body to cure itself by supplying it with curative force.

How to Read the Tarot
A Practical Method Using the Rider-Waite Deck

Discover Swami Nirmalananda's unique method of reading the Tarot specifically for use with the Rider-Waite deck, with detailed instructions on how to use the cards to develop your intuition for understanding the meanings of the cards. Illustrated with color plates of each of the cards of the Rider-Waite deck with full explanations of their symbolism.

More Titles

Light from Eternal Lamps

www.ingramcontent.com/pod-product-compliance
Lightning Source LLC
Chambersburg PA
CBHW032048040426
42449CB00007B/1026